Procrastination Cure

2 in 1

How to Stop Procrastinating, Live up to Your Full Potential and Succeed in Life: Includes Goal Setting Success and Productivity Plan

TIFFANY ADAMS

Copyright 2019 © Tiffany Adams

All rights reserved.

No part of this guide may be reproduced in any form without permission in writing from the publisher except in the case of review.

Legal & Disclaimer

This book is copyright protected. It is only for personal use. You cannot amend, distribute, sell, use, quote or paraphrase any part, or the content within this book, without the consent of the author or publisher.

Please note the information contained within this document is for educational and entertainment purposes only. All effort has been executed to present accurate, up to date, reliable, complete information. No warranties of any kind are declared or implied. Readers acknowledge that the author is not engaging in the rendering of legal, financial, medical or professional advice. The content within this book has been derived from various sources. Please consult a licensed professional before attempting any techniques outlined in this book.

By reading this document, the reader agrees that under no circumstances is the author responsible for any losses, direct or indirect, that are incurred as a result of the use of information contained within this document, including, but not limited to, errors, omissions, or inaccuracies.

Table of Contents

Book 1:
Goal Setting Success

How To Stop Procrastination, Improve Your Mental Focus, And Achieve Any Goal You Want in Life

Introduction

How to Win at Life—The Simple Way

All of us are searching for success. Perhaps we want to lose weight, start a business, or learn a new skill. Maybe we're on a quest for personal change. We want to be better parents, better children, and better citizens.

The thing is, we all want *something*.

The definition of success is different for each individual person. For example, an aspiring athlete might picture success differently than a stay-at-home mom. But in the end, no matter how we define it, we all want to reach our own definition of a good, successful life.

What if I told you that it is completely possible to reach your goals?

No matter how old you are, your financial situation, your life goals—there is a way to work your way to success. Many scientific studies, tons of psychological evidence, and countless stories have all backed this method up. Plus, it's something you can learn at any point in your life, and it only takes seven short steps to complete.

Why We Struggle to Set Goals

Not everyone considers themselves to be goal-oriented. In fact, some of us don't even like thinking about goals. Setting goals means we will eat tasteless, diet-friendly food; force ourselves to be friendly to people we don't really like; and wake up at ungodly hours to work on something that feels unattainable. Then we quit, without taking a closer look at our plan of action—if we made a plan of action at all. This can turn into a vicious cycle of wishing for change but avoiding any action.

People tend to be less likely to set goals if they are afraid of failing. They remember past New Year's resolutions and goals they had set and abandoned over the years. This psychological weight is where the process of goal setting turns into more of a mental game, and we will cover this more in-depth in the following chapters. For now, do your best to start working against these mental and psychological blocks today. Right now, take a moment to:

- Breathe in. Hold it. Count to three. Now breathe out. Deep breathing has been shown to clear the mind and help relieve stress. If you breathe deeply while setting your goals, you are teaching your brain to relax and become comfortable with thinking about your goals.

- Close your eyes and imagine how much happier your life will be when you complete that goal you've set for yourself. And remember, it's not "if," it's "when."

Sometimes, it's easy to like the idea of being

organized. You might think to yourself, "I'll be more organized when I finish this project at work," or "I'll be more organized when I retire." And often, people avoid setting goals because they believe they're not organized enough.

Don't put off your organization skills until tomorrow. According to studies done at the University College London, it can take anywhere from 18 to 254 days for a new habit to become part of your everyday routine. Organization and goal setting are both habits like brushing your teeth, and they will become easier the more you practice them.

In the next few chapters, I will show you how you can learn to organize your goals and stay on track, even when you hate setting goals. And of course, better organization is an excellent personal goal to work toward.

Procrastinator to Psychologist: My Journey to Success

My name is Tiffany Adams and I come from a family of chronic procrastinators. Growing up in my family, procrastination was normal and just another part of everyday life. I figured this was part of my personality makeup, and I would never be able to change it. These procrastination habits stayed with me all throughout my childhood, up until I attended college.

Once I focused on my goal of becoming a psychologist, my procrastination habits reappeared and were preventing me from success. Things got put off until the last second, projects and schoolwork became difficult to manage, and as the extra stress and worries piled up, I wondered, "How in the world can I become a successful psychologist if I continue procrastinating so much?"

At last, something clicked and I needed to change my approach. I realized that these habits couldn't continue, and I didn't want procrastination to become my downfall.

For a while, I did some research online and read books about how to change my habits and achieve my goals. Whenever I found a good resource, I tried to follow their guidelines and did my best to stop procrastinating, but nothing seemed to work. Their advice would help me for the first week or so, but they wouldn't stay for long. In no time, I was back to my old ways—procrastinating constantly.

I wanted to change but I had no idea how to stay motivated with my goals. It grew discouraging, and at times, I found myself thinking that there was nothing I could do. Perhaps I was born to be this way and I couldn't change myself.

However, with a little more research, I managed to find podcasts and motivational speakers that gave me the encouragement I needed to keep going. With their help and guidance, I started taking steps towards a more organized lifestyle, and over time, I managed to control procrastination habits and design better habits that worked for my lifestyle.

Today, I am a full time psychologist with a bachelor's degree in psychology. I have learned how to control my procrastination habits, and now I have the skills I need to fully pursue my goals.

After I saw what a huge difference goal setting made in my own life, I wanted to share this information with others, so I decided to write a book in which I could show other people how to retake control of their lives and strive for their goals. I wanted to write a book that made a positive impact on people's lives, and that's the book you're reading right now!

A Guide to Goal Setting Success

In this book, I'll be discussing some different strategies for setting and achieving your life goals. First of all, it's important to choose your goals wisely, so we'll discuss how to choose goals that fit your life vision. You will also find step-by-step guides for creating a plan of action, setting up an accountability network, and finding trustworthy mentors.

After choosing a primary goal to focus on, we need to build that plan of action. According to studies conducted at Dominican University, people who write down their goals are up to 33% more likely to succeed. In chapters 2 and 3, we'll break down your goal into easy-to-complete steps for you to practice in your day-to-day life and strategies to stick to with your goals. I have also addressed the topic of procrastination, because we all know it happens to the best of us, and it's important to learn how to overcome it.

I have designed this book to take you through the entire process of goal setting from start to finish. We will begin by evaluating your goals and deciding on a primary goal to focus on. After working through this book, you will be ready to celebrate! By then, you will have knowledge about the goal setting process that will serve you for the rest of your life.

So, let's go ahead and get started!

Chapter One: Choosing the Right Goals for Success

*What is a **goal**? If I have multiple goals, which one should I focus on first? How can I start achieving my goals?*

Everyone has goals, whether or not they consciously realize it, and if you are reading this book, chances are you already have some goals in mind. At least you have an idea of where you want to start heading in your fitness journey, your professional life, or your path of self-discovery. In this chapter, we will take a deeper look at your goals, then go through a step-by-step process to figure out which goals to focus on first.

Let's go ahead and dive into our first task.

List Your Goals

The first step in a book about goal setting success is, obviously, creating a list of everything you would like to accomplish in the near future. You don't have to go into large amounts of detail in this stage if you don't want to. For now, we will just brainstorm some different goals that you may have in your life.

Here are some ideas to get you started:

- What is your dream job? What qualifications do you need to get hired in this position?

- Do you consider yourself a humanitarian? Is there a way that you want to become more generous with your time? Consider goals like volunteering, donating more, and helping others that you come across in your daily life.

- Do you want to eat healthier? Are fast food meals putting a strain on your budget? Is there a safe, doctor-approved diet that you would like to start?

- Do you have an addiction that you haven't been able to kick yet? Is there anything you've become too dependent on?

- If you are in school, what are your goals as a student?

- Do you have any hobbies you would like to try out? What has prevented you from trying them in the past (time, finances)? What are some ways you can remove these barriers and try new things?

- How much extra money would you like to make per month? You could start your own business or side hustle.

- Do you say "yes" too often? Maybe you need to say "no" to things that aren't important to you and protect your time better. On the other hand, maybe you need to say "yes" more often and become more involved with your family and community.

- Do you struggle to stay close with your family? You could work on staying in touch with family members that live far away or focus on the members of your family that still live under your roof.

- Does your doctor recommend more exercise? Would you like to see yourself growing stronger and more sculpted? You could try running, power walking, weightlifting, or even yoga or tai chi.

- How do you want others to remember you? Is there something you consider to be your life's work? How can you build upon it and improve it?

Once you have a list of goals you would like to pursue, it's time to evaluate those goals. Let's take a look at some of the ways you can tell if a goal is a good fit for you.

Is This Goal a Good Fit?

It happens all the time: we make New Year's resolutions that we can't fulfill. According to Time Magazine, some New Year's resolutions that we break the most include travelling, losing weight, and getting out of debt, and while these are all good goals, they might not be the best goals for each individual person.

Now that we've finished examining the goal itself, let's take a quick look at your personality and lifestyle, and how they may affect the way you work on your goals.

Your Personality

Are you an organized person, or do you prefer to fly by the seat of your pants? Most of the time, more abstract goals are better for people who love organization. The task of splitting the goal into steps is practically second nature to them.

Of course, your goal might be to develop your organization skills. However, if you tend to do things on the spur of the minute, you'll probably do best with goals that apply to your daily routine and have a clear moment of success. For example, if you consider yourself to be less organized in your daily life, and you want to start eating healthier, your goal might be to cut back on the amount of calories you consume. So to do that, you could stop eating snacks in between meals. If the goal impacts your daily routine more than your personality, a goal like that one may be easier to remember. We will be exploring more about organization in chapters 2 and 3.

Goals affecting your personality (such as "I want to be more patient") are usually harder to achieve if you struggle with staying focused on one task at a time. To consciously change how you act requires a lot of effort. Of course, by using different strategies, anyone can achieve this type of goal, though it might be a good idea to work on staying focused and intentional before working on a personality-based goal. Don't forget to apply the SMARTY acronym and fix your goal accordingly.

Should You Focus on a Different Goal Instead?

Even if a goal is a good one to have, it might not be good for you.

Let me explain—let's say that Emily is a professional and a mother of two small children. She wakes up at six o'clock every morning, folds the laundry, throws in another load of towels, and gets the kids ready for school. Then, she heads to work where she spends most of the day in a cubicle, filling out spreadsheets and answering phone calls. When she gets home, she cooks dinner, feeds the kids, helps them with their homework, and then crashes in front of the television set for a few hours before she falls asleep on the couch. She only gets a couple hours of sleep, and it slows her down at work. It's hard for Emily to find some time to rest in her busy life.

However, instead of trying to find time to take care of herself, Emily decides that she needs to be a better employee so she can climb the corporate ladder to her dream job. She wants to spend more time at the office with the hopes that she will receive that promotion. She spends her entire day at the office, and when she comes home, she keeps thinking about the projects she has to finish. She doesn't give herself a chance to rest and recover from her day.

Even though her goal is good by itself, it might not be the best fit for this moment in her life. That doesn't mean she should stop working hard at her job; it simply means that she should focus on something else first. Right now, Emily needs to focus on taking better care of herself and her schedule before focusing so much time and energy on her career. Once she has her time management skills under control, and her sleep schedule improves, she will have a better chance at successfully getting her dream job.

Again, I do want to emphasize that Emily should continue doing well at her job. In the future, once she is getting enough sleep, Emily can go back to focusing on her career goals. However, to do well in her career, she needs to take care of her health first.

In this way, even if a goal is a good goal, it might not be right for you at the current time.

A Note About Peer Pressure

Is this goal something you heard about from someone else? Take a moment to think about all the media you consume on a regular basis, including books, magazines, music, movies, Netflix, Instagram, Facebook, Twitter, YouTube. Any one of these platforms can give you access to ideas and beliefs from anyone and anywhere in the world. Now, consider when you first thought about this goal. Did you first consider losing weight when your doctor recommended it, or did you wish you looked more like your favorite celebrities?

Peer pressure is a powerful tool that can either harm or help you, depending on how you use it. Negative peer pressure is something we all know about, and it's never a good idea to make life decisions based purely on peer pressure and other people's opinions.

Sure, it's a good idea to listen to the advice of loved ones and other people who care about your health, as peer pressure can be something you can leverage and turn in your favor. The most common ways to use positive peer pressure include building an accountability system and finding mentors, both of which we will discuss more in chapter 2.

Avoiding The Checklist Mindset

Sooner or later, most of us start viewing our goals as nothing more than a giant checklist of things we have to do, and in the process, we stop looking at the big picture. Many of us start on our goals by envisioning a checklist in our heads with the mentality of, "If I do these things, I will be successful."

While it is true that checklists are extremely helpful in goal setting, it's important to remember *why* you're working on this goal. No matter what goal you're working toward, if your motivation is in the right place, your ultimate goal is to improve your own life or the life of someone else. As humans, we all want to improve our lives, and it's part of our psyche to do so. This form of thinking that brought us to the point we're at today.

Keep in mind as we work through this book that your life is more than a checklist. You are not a number—you're a human being. Your life is not a checklist; it's your life, and you can take that life in any direction you choose.

This is why you need to remember to focus on your intentions, not just your checklist. This is the only life you'll ever get on this Earth, and you don't want to spend the rest of it marking off tasks. Checklists are supposed to help you through life, but do not let them control your life.

While we use checklists to remember our goals and measure how we can achieve them, we cannot make them the only way to chase our goals. Your intention should always be more important than the checklist. It's okay to take a break from it and focus on the big picture; in fact, I highly recommend taking a step back every once in a while to reevaluate where you're at, where you've been, and what you want your life to look like in the future. Doing this can help you discover the things you can work on that will impact your life as a whole and set goals based on those things.

Use the SMARTY Acronym

An easy way to evaluate your goals is to see if they fit with the **SMARTY** acronym. Many life coaches and professionals have used SMARTY to evaluate their goals and see if these goals are worth pursuing. There are many variations of this acronym, but we will stick with the following one for now.

SMARTY stands for **Specific**, **Measurable**, **Attainable**, **Relevant**, **Time-Oriented**, and **whY**.

- **Specific**: Is your goal specific enough? It's a good thing to say you want to be a better spouse, parent, child, or sibling, but it doing so can create vagueness that could also make your goal difficult to achieve. If your goal is more abstract right now, don't worry—we will cover how to focus your goals in the next few chapters.

- **Measurable**: How do you know when you've reached your goal? Picture the moment when you know you have achieved your goal. What does that look like for you?

For example, in Emily's situation, she might measure her health goals with getting at least eight hours of sleep every night for two weeks. Setting a standard like that makes it easy to tell when she has met her goal. Some goals, such as weight loss, are easier to measure while other goals might take more thought.

- **<u>A</u>ttainable**: Can you actually reach your goal? Whether you're an optimist or a pessimist, you need to step back and ask yourself this question with honesty. There's nothing wrong with dreaming of fame and fortune, but most of us cannot attain those goals with a few simple steps. If your goal might be unreachable, break it down into smaller chunks and focus on the individual steps. Again, we will discuss this in more detail later.

- **<u>R</u>elevant**: Will this goal impact the direction of your life? Is this impact positive? A goal like "quit smoking" will have an incredible impact on your life's direction, but a goal like "get a tattoo" probably won't change the course of your life too much.

There's not a right or wrong way to answer this question, unless your goal might have a negative impact in your life. In these cases, it would probably be best to avoid this sort of goal.

- **Time-Oriented**: What is your deadline? According to speaker Brian Tracy, deadlines can increase your chances of success by up to 11.5 times. Is your goal attached to a deadline? If not, can you create a deadline for your goal? Be sure to leave enough time to complete the goal, but don't give yourself six months when you only need one week. If a deadline is too far away, it won't motivate you to finish.

- **Y (Why)**: Why do you want to meet this goal? What motivates you? Is the motivation coming from yourself or the people closest to you? Be wary of when you are making goals from peer pressure. These goals often won't fit your lifestyle and have the potential to make you miserable. If your motivation is coming from both yourself and your inner circle, congratulations! That is the basis for a strong support group when you begin working toward your goal.

If you consider how your goal fits the SMARTY formula, you could probably tell if your goal is a good one to consider. It's important to trust your gut instincts on the matter.

It's also okay to take a loose approach to goal setting. If you know that your style is different than SMARTY, don't worry! You can still achieve your goals, just like everyone else. These are just some ideas to keep in mind as you evaluate your plans.

Prioritize Your Goals

Now that we have looked at some different ways to evaluate your goals, let's focus on how to prioritize your goals to narrow the focus onto only one or two. Without prioritizing, it's easy to become overwhelmed by goals and dreams, and when it becomes too overwhelming, people often quit working on their goals and think of themselves as failures. Of course they aren't failures; they simply didn't take the time to list their priorities.

For the sake of this example, let's say you're starting with four goals in mind, and you have no idea which goals to prioritize. The following is a simple way to prioritize your goals.

Grab a pencil and paper and write down your list of goals in this order:

- First, if any of your goals have to do with a **medical issue,** a doctor's recommendation, or from others who are genuinely concerned about your health, this goal is your number one priority. Taking care of yourself should always come first, especially if you have struggled with your health for a while. You should place any goals in this category at the top of the list.

- Next, list any **goals that you've been wanting to achieve for a while**, but haven't gotten around to yet. The longer this goal has been on your mind, the more likely you are to finish it. It's important to you, and maybe you even attempted it in the past (note that it's a good thing to pick up past goals and try them again, because you will now have a better understanding of what your personal roadblocks are, and you'll be more prepared to overcome them).

- After that, list the **goals that are important to you**, but you're not sure yet if it's the right goal for you. We'll put these ideas "on hold," so if you decide to come back to them, they will be there, but they may not be super important in your life right now.

- Finally, add any goals that might be a **good idea** to work towards in the future. One example would be if you are a college student and you want to eventually become a parent or travel the world. Be creative with this section and don't hold back. These are the goals that you want to keep in your subconscious, but perhaps you're not in a position to pursue them right now.

At this point, if you want to rearrange the goals, feel free to do so. No matter what, you will start by tackling the goals in the top two spots of your list first.

How to Make Your Goals Concrete

Let's take a look at how to take your top goals from ideas to concrete goals that fit every part of the SMARTY acronym. To start, we need to take goals that might be a bit vague and turn them into something we can define.

There's nothing wrong with abstract goals. In fact, it's a good idea to keep these sorts of goals in the back of your mind and allow your subconscious to absorb them. Usually, these goals include plans to "be a nicer sibling," "conquer my procrastination," or "get better at managing my temper." They are goals that don't have a definite end when you can check them off your list.

These are often noble goals that include a lot of different factors and often, the easiest way to succeed with them is to split them into smaller subgoals. Let's look at a couple of examples.

Mary has always struggled with procrastination. She can't ever get anything done because she's always putting it off for later, focusing on other things, and making excuses to herself. She sees that doing so is affecting her life in many ways, so she wants to do something to change it. Instead of focusing on the big goal (procrastination), Mary decides to break it up into smaller pieces, including things like "stop piling stuff on my desk" (she often procrastinates about cleaning) and "spend less time on my computer" (so she won't procrastinate so much online). By breaking her big goal into subgoals, Mary has a better chance of procrastinating less.

Dave wants to be a better father to his teenage daughters. He's trying to figure out how to stay close to his daughters throughout their adolescence, and he's not really sure how to start. So, instead of saying something vague like "I want to be a perfect dad," Dave focuses on three smaller subgoals: going out with his daughters once a month for a father-daughter date, asking them every day about their lives, and telling them "I love you" every night. There could be many other potential subgoals that Dave could focus on, but these ones are an excellent starting point. They are also time-oriented because he wants these goals to become habits.

Notice that subgoals are not individual steps, and we will talk about making a list of steps for your goal in the next chapter. Subgoals are individual goals of their own. Mary might need to take several steps to reach her subgoals, but she will have a much easier time accomplishing these subgoals than trying to tackle her procrastination as a whole. Dave will probably not be a perfect dad after accomplishing his subgoals, but he will be a better dad than he was when he started. Subgoals help you make progress on large scale goals that you can't accomplish all at once.

If your goal is large scale or abstract, it's a good idea to take some time to pinpoint why you want to work on that goal. You can build subgoals to conquer the symptoms of a larger problem. Let's say you want to work on controlling your anger. You would focus on the symptoms of that problem; for example, you could focus on walking away from the problem, not shouting, and calming down instead of getting angry in public.

Right now, take a few minutes and **brainstorm at least five different subgoals** you can focus on. Then, save this list for future reference, as you will be referencing it in the future.

Setting Deadlines that Work

Ah, deadlines. Most of us hate it when we have a big deadline looming over us, but according to some studies, deadlines could mean the difference between failure and success. In a study conducted by Dan Ariely of the Massachusetts Institute of Technology, if people are aware that they struggle with procrastination, self-assigned deadlines are a strategic way to keep yourself focused on a task. And of course, deadlines from outside forces such as bosses, teachers, and others have shown to be even more effective because you have someone to hold you accountable.

Your goal might have a built-in deadline; for example, if your goal is to earn better test grades, your deadline will be the day when you take the test. In most cases, however, it's important to set up your own deadline or even more than one deadline to make sure you keep your goals on track.

To create deadlines that will help you stay productive, be sure to:

- Give yourself enough time to complete the project, but not much more. If you only need two weeks to finish your goal, don't give yourself three months. The deadline will lose its power and you'll inevitably spend most of those three months procrastinating, which is not good.

- Allow a little bit of wiggle room for mistakes. Life happens at the most inconvenient times, and in the case of an emergency or some other inescapable event, you'll be glad to have an extra day or two. Again, don't give yourself too much time, but it's a good idea to stay realistic and remember that things might come up while you're in the middle of chasing your goals.

- Write down your goal. Get creative with this one—you could design notes to hang on your mirror or decorate the deadline day on your calendar. Allow yourself to get excited about it! By this date, you will be well on your way to success and you will be successfully achieving your goals.

A good deadline will encourage you, not overwhelm you. I believe in the importance of deadlines. They have been proven to shake your procrastination and make it easier for you to get stuff done, which is how you will achieve success.

How to Create a Deadline

What should you do if your goal doesn't have a deadline yet? There are several ways to come up with a deadline, and we'll take a closer look at some of the ones that will motivate you to succeed.

I consider deadlines to be an art form—all right, maybe not quite to that extent, but I do find them to be quite helpful in my goal-setting. Without deadlines, nothing would ever get done, and we would never stop procrastinating.

The first step in setting a deadline for yourself is to take a look at your productivity patterns. Do you tend to accomplish more on Mondays when the week is fresh, or on Thursdays and Fridays when the week is wrapping up? A good rule of thumb for deadlines is to place the deadline right *after* your peak of productivity. This means that if you work best at the beginning of the week, putting your deadline on a Wednesday means that you can take advantage of your productive nature on Mondays.

You always want to allow for a final creative push right before the deadline, so try to schedule your deadline with this in mind. If the days before your deadline are filled up with other obligations, you won't have much energy to dedicate to your goal, right when you need energy the most. It's best to keep the days before your deadline as open as possible.

Beyond that, your deadline completely depends on you, your schedule, and the type of goal you set. Below, I've listed a couple of examples of common goals and their sample deadlines to give you some ideas. Feel free to build off of these as needed.

- **Goal: Lily wants to work out more.**

Deadline: To reach a deadline on this one, Lily should be more specific. Let's say she breaks her goal down into "run a mile in eight minutes." Lily can't quite run a mile yet, but she can run about half a mile comfortably, so her first subgoal is to run a mile. Then, she can focus on improving her speed. After this, she might decide that her deadline is in three months, or less if she's disciplined enough.

- **Goal**: Kevin wants to learn guitar.

  Deadline: Kevin might be taking a class at a community center, which runs for two or three months. or he might teach himself at home using YouTube videos. This is a good goal to accomplish fairly quickly, so his deadline could be in four or five weeks, depending on how many hours he spends practicing.

- **Goal**: Maria wants to become a veterinarian.

  Deadline: If Maria is fresh out of high school, she can count on four years of undergraduate studies and then four years of specialized graduate school. Her ultimate deadline is in eight years. Of course, along the way, she will have many subgoals, all of which contain their own deadlines. Maria's goal includes making it into vet school, which is quite competitive, so she must meet the deadlines provided by the school. She will also need to use deadlines to keep on top of her undergraduate studies.

If you have absolutely no clue how far in advance to set your deadline, try searching for some pointers online or ask your friends and family for their advice. Goals can take anywhere from a few days to several years to complete, depending on the goal and your personality.

After You Meet the Deadline

Take a moment to imagine the moment when you meet your deadline and finish your goal. Doesn't it feel empowering? It's like looking back down at the ground after having climbed a mountain and realizing how far you've come. You've conquered your goals, and now it's time to celebrate!

The best part about completing a huge task is that you have a chance to celebrate your accomplishments. You just did something you may have never done before! You sacrificed, sweated, and slaved over this goal, and now, if you've faithfully stuck to your action plan, you have finally achieved your goals.

In this moment, how do you plan to celebrate?

Planning a reward for yourself is almost as important as coming up with a deadline. Without a reward, your brain can lose interest in your goals. You don't want to give yourself a reward that works against your goals (a tub of ice cream is not a good reward for eating healthy). Take this time to come up with a reward that you can use to keep your brain motivated.

Is there a show that you like to watch? Maybe the producers are about to come out with a new season, and you've been dying to see it.

Is there a place near your hometown that you'd like to spend a day at? Short day trips can make excellent rewards because it doesn't include the price tag of a large-scale vacation, but you still get a chance to get out of town and see something that you haven't seen in a while.

Some more ideas include getting a massage, buying a new book you've been eyeing for a while, taking a day off, visiting a museum, or simply sleeping in late the next morning. As long as your reward doesn't contradict your goals or ruin your health permanently, go ahead and get creative. When you achieve that goal, you will make time for this celebration, and it will feel amazing!

Chapter Two:
Building an Action Plan

So, you have a list of goals that you would like to work on. No matter if you've run all of them through the SMARTY test or not, even if your goals are still just some ideas floating around in your head, it's all okay. We will take those goals and get them out of your head and onto a piece of paper, shaping them into an action plan that will help you start chipping away at them.

Every person's action plan will be unique, as it should be. There is no such thing as a "one size fits all" action plan because everyone works in their own distinctive way. Kylie works better with spur-of-the-minute decisions while Brian writes one checklist and nothing more and Robert prefers to organize his goals with lots of checklists and planners. These are all equally valid ways of working, and not one of them is better than the others.

Maybe you see yourself more like Kylie in our example. You can't stand the idea of confining yourself to a specific schedule, and you definitely can't see yourself sitting down and writing a full-length action plan for anything because planners and schedules are for losers. If you find yourself agreeing with these statements, you might do best with a **Loose Action Sketch Plan**.

The Loose Action Sketch Plan

When you don't find any joy in scheduling your time or activities, you shouldn't force yourself to create an elaborate plan to outline each of your goals. It's not realistic to put this expectation on yourself because you have already planned to focus so much energy on meeting your goals. You don't want to drain your energy by setting up too many schedules and checklists. **The Loose Action Sketch Plan (LASP)** is an easy way to think about your goals and lay down some ground rules for achieving them. For the sake of this chapter, I'll go ahead and assume that you already have some idea of what your goals are. We will focus on your main goal for now.

To start piecing together a LASP, you need a vision. If you're not big on detailed action plans, you need to constantly focus on the big picture. What do you want to accomplish? How does this goal fit into the big picture of your life in general?

One idea to help focus your mind on the big picture is to create a **vision board**. This can be anything from a Pinterest board to an entire wall of your bedroom; although, most people like to use bulletin boards because they're easier to move and they aren't digital, so you can see your vision board at all times, even when your internet is slow. If your goal is to save enough money for a new car, your vision board might include pictures of the specific car you want to buy, pictures of the car's interior, clip art of money bags, and anything else that reminds you of your goal: to save enough money to buy that car.

Another aspect of the LASP is to draw or write a flowchart for yourself. Yes, it's a plan, but it isn't as strenuous as it sounds. All you need to do is grab a paper and pencil, pen, crayon, or whatever writing tool that inspires you. Turn the paper so it's horizontal; at one end, draw a stick figure to represent yourself, and at the other end of the paper, write down your goal. It should look like a skeleton sketch of a timeline. How can you plan to get from point A to point B? It's okay if you genuinely can't think of anything, but if you have some ideas, write or draw them in the space between you and your goal. Unlike a timeline, don't worry too much about these ideas being in any specific order. Spread them out all over the page, as doing so can help keep your brain from seeing it as a schedule or organized list.

When you finish your flowchart, you have a choice to make. You can either add it to your vision board or jot down the best ideas from the flowchart onto a Post-it note, then rip your flowchart into shreds and throw it away. Yes, I said you could throw it away. If goal setting planners and checklists have discouraged you in the past, go ahead and throw away that flowchart. You've gotten some ideas, but you won't define yourself with this piece of paper. It's just a diving board or a jumping-off point.

At this point, you should have your vision board and your flowchart, which may or may not be in the depths of your trash can. The last thing you should set up at this point is your deadline reminders. As we discussed in the previous chapter, you should always have a deadline for your goals to help overcome your procrastination.

You want to keep your deadline in the back of your mind, but it's not a good idea to stress about it all the time, no matter what your work style is. Especially for people who work best with loose schedules, you shouldn't make the deadline your main focus, even though it will be present. A good way to do this is to set yourself some reminders on your phone. Depending on how far away your deadline is, you can set reminders for one month, one week, two days, and one day before the deadline. Many people have found this system to be efficient, as it reminds them they have a deadline, but it doesn't hinder their process and workflow.

In summary, for a reliable LASP, consider the following steps:

- Create a vision board that inspires you to focus on the big picture.

- Sketch out a basic flowchart for yourself and throw it away if you want to.

- Set reminders for your deadline.

Once you have your LASP in mind, stick around. We will discuss the details of finding accountability partners and mentors later in this chapter. Let's go ahead and move on to our next topic: creating action plans for people who like to plan some of their steps in advance.

Action Plans for Relaxed Planners

In our brief example of different planning personalities, Kylie doesn't like scheduling her work, Brian schedules his time when he has an important project he's working on, and Robert loves organizing every minute of his day. We just looked at some ways that people like Kylie can focus on their vision and create a loose action plan, so now, we will move on and take a look at how people like Brian can get started with a basic action plan.

The first step is to identify your planner of choice. Different people work better with different styles of planners. For example, people who check their schedule multiple times per day will usually do well with a spiral-bound planner that they can take to work. People who plan out their day in advance tend to prefer wall calendars, so they can check their schedule in the morning and not have to worry about checking a planner throughout the day.

Maybe you have a specific system you like to use to keep track of your schedule. For the sake of our example, we'll say that Brian enjoys using his phone calendar to keep track of his appointments. It's handy and easy to use, but it doesn't require the commitment of a detailed goal planner.

Once you decide how you will record your action plan, whether you use a calendar or a planner, it's time to outline your action plan. I highly recommend finding a piece of paper and a pencil to work through the next few steps, as writing by hand can help boost your memory.

To begin, write your goal across the top of the page, then start thinking of the steps you'll need to take to achieve this goal. Here are a couple of examples to help you get started:

- Michelle wants to quit her job and start working as a full time freelancer. To reach this goal, she decides to apply for at least five freelance jobs per week for three weeks. She breaks this step down even further—to apply for those jobs, she needs to update her resume, schedule some time to set up her own website, and improve her interview skills.

- Greg wants to volunteer more. To reach his goal, he decides to research some different nonprofits who are looking for volunteers. He also cuts back the hours he spends watching television, so when he finds somewhere to volunteer, he' will have some time in his schedule.

For more tips on creating steps and subgoals, be sure to take a look back at chapter one: how to make your goals concrete. Once you have a list of the steps you'll need to take to reach your goals, we will talk a little bit about bullet journals, planners, and which one can fit best with your personality and goals.

A Brief Introduction to Bullet Journaling

In recent years, **bullet journaling** has become the planner of choice for thousands of people worldwide. According to the creator of the bullet journal Ryder Carroll, the bullet journal method is meant to bring mindfulness into a productivity system. After being diagnosed with learning disabilities, Carroll developed the bullet journal method as a way to organize his time, and it wasn't long before his system became hugely popular among people of all ages.

He did not mean for bullet journaling to be overly difficult, and it really isn't. While there are various books about bullet journaling, we will discuss how you can use a bullet journal to keep track of your goals.

To begin, you will need a journal. On the first two pages, you'll keep your notebook index and a code for the symbols you decide to use, that is, if you decide to use symbols to organize your ideas. Within your bullet journal, you can include calendar pages, goal pages, bucket list pages, and even pages where you track your mood over the course of the year. For ideas on how to create stunning bullet journals, you can look up some bullet journal ideas on Pinterest.

To set up a bullet journal for one specific goal, the key is to take several approaches and focus on the reason why you want this goal. For example, let's say Cara wants to be a better mom, which is a multi-faceted goal that involves a lot of steps. In her bullet journal, Cara could include:

- An index page (like a table of contents)

- A "Mommy Bucket List" page in which she doodles and jots down all the things she wants to be as a mother (she draws a heart, a steaming muffin, and an open door to symbolize that she wants to be welcoming to friends and family). This list describes the reasons why she wants to be a better mom.

- A mood tracker in which she tracks how she feels about her parenting skills (green means it was a standard day, blue means she feels she can't handle her children, pink means she lost her temper at least twice). This page can help her visualize her parenting habits and how she might change them. For example, over two months, Cara sees a lot of blue on her mood tracker, so she might want to look into new parenting styles that can help her learn how to discipline her kids.

- A goal checklist of things to do every day (Cara wants to hug her kids twice a day, say "I love you" twice a day, and spend time talking with them at least once a day.)

There is no right or wrong way to bullet journal, so I encourage you to look at some examples and ideas online and give it a shot. You might discover that it's not a good fit for you, or you could discover that you absolutely love it. You won't know until you try it out.

Now, let's talk a little bit about using a checklist or a flowchart to organize your goals.

Using a Checklist

For those who don't consider themselves artsy, bullet journaling might not be an enjoyable experience, especially if you feel pressure to keep up with the bullet journals that people post on Pinterest. While you should never give up on something because someone online does it better, if something's truly not your style, don't force yourself to do something that doesn't fit your personality.

Let's take a look at Brian, the guy in our earlier example. On our spectrum of organized schedules, Brian falls in the middle in between Kylie (who hates planning anything in advance) and Robert (who plans every aspect of his day, so he doesn't miss anything). Brian is just an average guy working a nine-to-five in Los Angeles, and he wants to start meeting his goals for the future. However, he's not sure how to remind himself of his goals.

Since Brian is in the middle, his approach should consist of a mix between Kylie's vision board and Robert's schedules. Brian shouldn't let himself forget about the big picture, but he also needs to plan out his steps so he can keep himself on track.

The simplest strategy for Brian (and others who classify themselves in this category) may be to stick with a simple checklist and vision board combo. This will ensure that people who think like Brian can get the best of both worlds, even if they don't enjoy bullet journaling.

Using the list of steps and subgoals that we created earlier, let's go ahead and turn that into a checklist by breaking down each step as far as we possibly can. We'll say that Brian wants to learn how to sail, and one of the steps he came up with was to take a class. We can break that step down even further by splitting it into three parts: call the class instructor and decide if it's a good class, pay the registration fee, and make sure that he's open on that day so he can go to the sailing class. Then we can keep breaking them down even more. Calling the class instructor can't happen unless Brian has the right phone number, so he needs to track down the instructor's phone number first.

Once you have broken down the checklist into the simplest steps, go ahead and write the final draft of your checklist on a clean sheet of paper. Feel free to decorate it a little bit with doodles or fancy lettering. The more eye-catching it is, the better.

Next, it's time to hang up the checklist. Some people like to write notes to themselves and tape them to their bathroom mirror; however, I don't recommend this, because the steam from your shower could cause the ink on your notes to bleed. I've found that the best place to put important papers is to hang it at eye level next to your bedroom door. That way, you'll see it when you wake up every morning. You could also try hanging your checklist next to the place where you keep your keys.

In addition to checklists, try creating a basic flowchart for yourself to chronicle your journey towards your goals.

Flowcharts and How to Use Them

The technical definition of a **flowchart** is a diagram that illustrates a process or work flow. In simpler terms, it's an illustrated version of your checklist. A flowchart is a simple way to change the way you view your goals. It focuses on the "if/then" statements, such as "if I buy cheaper coffee, then I will have more money to spend on that Disneyland trip" or "if I meditate every day, then my stress levels will go down."

To create a flowchart, take a clean sheet of paper and write your first and smallest step at the top. Then, continue listing different steps and approaches, following the "if/then" pattern until you reach your goal or subgoal.

Flowcharts aren't that much different from checklists, so we will go ahead and move on to the next section. If you're interested in learning more about flowcharts, I recommend doing some research on flowcharts online or at your local library.

What If I Still Don't Know What to Do?

So far, we've discussed how to create a loose action plan using vision boards and simple flowcharts. We also talked about bullet journaling, creating and using checklists, and about the topic of flowcharts.

Now, if you're still not sure which planning style fits you, it probably means you are more like Brian. Try out a few ideas from this chapter for yourself and see which ones work for you currently and which ones you can see yourself doing six months from now. You're welcome to mix and match ideas however you want—as discussed, there is no cut and dry way to plan out your goals.

There was a reason we did not discuss Robert, the guy in our example who loves schedules and planners. Since he loves his schedule so much, It is safe to assume that he already knows how to schedule his time, and he probably has a favorite planner as well. If you consider yourself an organized planner like Robert, but you still don't have a favorite planner, I recommend exploring the following options:

- Spiral-bound planners (usually consists of a calendar and pages to write notes on).

- Wall calendars (easy to hang in places where you'll look at them every day, such as the kitchen, office, or next to the TV).

- Excel spreadsheets (completely digital and easy to adjust).

Once you have some ideas for organizing your goals and the steps you'll take to achieve them, it's time to move on to something even more important than schedules—accountability.

The All-in-One Guide to Accountability Partners

For some of us, the idea of accountability partners makes us think that we're doing something wrong, like we need a parent to oversee us and make sure that we won't mess up or get in trouble. However, this could not be farther from the truth.

Accountability partners are the most honest and trustworthy support system. They will ask you how your progress is going, what your next steps are, and they'll double check that you're on track to meet your goals by the deadline. They can offer a shoulder to cry on and a gigantic cheer when you finally accomplish your goal. They will also be invested in checking your progress.

An accountability partner is anyone you respect who can keep you focused on reaching your goals in the most efficient way possible. The person you choose to keep you accountable should be willing and able to check in with you, and they will expect you to report to them truthfully. They must be someone that you can be 100% honest with, even when you mess up.

Every goal needs at least one accountability partner. Studies conducted by the American Society of Training and Development found that people have a 65% success rate of achieving their goals after adding an accountability partner. When people scheduled regular meetings with their accountability partners, their success rate increased to a whopping 95%! That means that the people who found accountability partners and met with those partners on a regular basis achieved their goals 95% of the time. Those are some significant numbers that you don't want to overlook.

There are a lot of different people you might ask to be your accountability partner. Here are some people you might ask to be your accountability partner, starting with family and friends.

- Your spouse, if you're married, or your significant other. However, it might not be best to ask your boyfriend or girlfriend to be your accountability partner when you've only gone out on two dates with them.

- Your parents, whether or not you still live with them.

- Your siblings, as long as they are mature and dependable.

- Any close friends in your life whom you can have deep conversations with. The friends who never talk about deep topics are probably not a good choice because they may not have the maturity required to be an accountability partner. If you're struggling with your goals, you will want accountability partners who will be kind but firm and telling you how to get back on track.

- A leader of your church or other religious group. Religion offers community that focuses on helping others. Perhaps there is a pastor or leader whom you look up to that might be willing to be your accountability partner. This works especially well if your goals are spiritually based.

- A therapist.

- A business partner or financial advisor, if your goal has to do with business.

Keep in mind that an accountability partner is different from a mentor. We'll talk about mentors later, but for now, make sure you recognize the differences. The following points outline the differences between a mentor and an accountability partner.

- Accountability partners ask you what you're doing to achieve your goals; mentors will tell you how to achieve your goals.

- Accountability partners are usually more of a support system; mentors act more as if a business-like relationship (not in every case, but most of the time).

- Accountability partners are there to keep you on the right track; mentors will help you build the tracks.

To ask someone to be your accountability partner is super simple. Just explain your goals to them and ask if they would be willing to help keep you on track. Let's look at an example dialogue really quick between Ryan and his dad. Ryan wants to quit smoking, and he wants to ask his dad to be an accountability partner for him.

Ryan might say something like, "Dad, you know that I've been smoking for about five years. I've decided that I want to quit smoking, but I know it's not going to be easy. If I start the process of quitting, would you be willing to check in with me and hold me accountable?"

He could also be more abrupt: "Dad, I'm going to quit smoking this year. Would you be willing to be my accountability partner?"

Either way, if he has a good relationship with his dad, his dad will probably be glad to help him out.

There's also nothing wrong with having more than one accountability partner! Two or three accountability partners at once can help you stay focused even more. And of course, when you achieve your goals, you'll want to have some people to celebrate with.

When you do find an accountability partner, how do you plan to keep in touch with them? The most obvious choice is with face-to-face contact. Go grab coffee with them or take them for a hike or a trip to the mall, as long as you're okay with discussing your goal within earshot of other people. In some cases, however, you may live too far apart or you don't have the time to meet up. Facetime and Skype calls are excellent alternatives if you can't meet your potential partner face-to-face. You could also talk on the phone once a week and check in with them, so long as you remain absolutely honest about your progress and the struggles you're facing.

Accountability partners will help you stay focused and offer encouragement when the going gets tough. If you pick your accountability partners wisely, they can make all the difference. Be sure to thank them for their time and show them how much you appreciate their help.

Once you have accountability partners in place, go ahead and move on to the next step: selecting a mentor.

Selecting a Mentor

Mentors are the best way to make sure you're still on track to achieve your goals. Your mentor can be anyone you look up to and preferably someone who has already succeeded in meeting goals similar to yours. For example, if you're looking for someone to mentor you in your physical fitness, you could hire a professional trainer, or you could spend time with your mom's friend's husband who competed in the Iron Man competition two years ago. The person you learn from should have experience in the areas you want to succeed in.

An obvious choice for a mentor is a paid professional who makes a living by mentoring people in your exact situation. These professionals might include nutritionists, fitness trainers, and therapists. Another option is to approach someone who works in the field or position that you would like to work in someday.

The first step in finding a mentor is to keep it simple. You don't want to make the conversation awkward by barging into the person's office and demanding they help you out, unless you're paying a professional (if you're dealing with a professional mentor figure, they probably already know you want their help and advice; however, you should still speak politely).

Most of the time, the best way to begin a mentor relationship with someone is to ask, "Can I take you out for coffee?" Who's going to say no to this offer? When you do get a chance to meet with them, take some time and get to know more about their personalities, their goals, and their lives. This first meeting is a little bit like a first date; you don't want to "pop the question" just yet.

Of course, there are some cases that might be a little different. In the case where the person you're asking is a family member, a friend, or even a teacher, you could probably ask them right away, "Could you be my mentor?"

Let's look at a couple of examples. Laura wants to go back to college after five years of raising her children. She can meet with a university counselor from her local college, and she decides to ask him about her financial aid options. Even though this might not be considered a mentoring relationship, the university counselor can help Laura achieve her goal, which is to go back to college. The counselor won't be able to help with any other aspects of Laura's life, but it is still a great idea for Laura to meet with him anyway. He is a mentor in one aspect of Laura's goals— that is, to get back into college.

Greg wants to build his business. He might seek out someone he knows in the industry, or if nothing else, he can ask his friends and family if they know anyone who is successful in business. Once he finds someone he would like to talk to, he should take them out for coffee and ask them about their story: how they got started, how they get their work done, and where they want to be in the next five years. After meeting with this person two or three times, Greg can talk to them about why he needs guidance and ask if they would be willing to give him some advice. It's up to Greg whether or not to explain that he's looking for a mentor.

Cheng is looking to strengthen his marriage. The best mentor for Cheng would be someone who has been married for a long time, preferably for several decades. He might find this person at church, temple, or another religious meeting, or they may simply be one of Cheng's grandparents. When he finds a suitable mentor, he can take them out to lunch and explain that he's looking for their marriage advice, and he would be honored if they took some time to mentor him. Most of the time, senior citizens are happy to share their advice with someone younger than them, so Cheng can ask the question up front without sounding abrupt.

To summarize, a mentor is someone who can help you figure out how to approach a problem. They are best described as a coach who wants to help you achieve your goal in the best way possible, and they will have lots of experience in the field that you're interested in. You want to be like this person someday.

Once you have someone who is willing to be a mentor figure for you, you're ready to get started taking your first steps towards success.

Chapter Three: Taking Your First Steps To Success

Now that we have our goals, accountability partners, and mentors in place, it's time to take the first steps toward success. In the past two chapters, you outlined some of the steps and subgoals that will help you get closer to meeting your goal, so let's take a look at how we can take those steps and turn them into reality.

If you have already broken down your steps and subgoals, your list might look like this:

Goal = Lose thirty pounds before June 21st.

- Start working out every day

  - ❖ Sign up for a personal trainer

  - ❖ Wake up at 6 AM every weekday and go to the gym

  - ❖ Build a playlist of motivating workout music

- Eat healthier

  - ❖ Follow the Ketogenic diet for three months

  - ❖ Avoid sugar and alcohol

This list is broken down well; however, if we want to, we can break it down even further into something like this:

- Start working out every day

  - ❖ Sign up for a personal trainer

  - ❖ Wake up at 6 AM every weekday and go to the gym

    - o Set alarm clock for 6 AM

    - o Make sure workout clothes are washed and ready to wear every morning

    - o Text Mindy and see if she wants to go workout together

  - ❖ Build a playlist of motivating workout music

    - o Listen to Pandora and Spotify on the way to work to find songs to work out to

- Eat healthier

❖ Follow the Ketogenic diet for three months

  o Go to the library and find books about the Keto diet

  o Research easy keto recipes on Pinterest (find at least twenty)

  o Create a shopping list of ingredients

  o Go to the grocery store and buy the basic ingredients for a keto meal plan

❖ Avoid sugar and alcohol

  o On the vacation to New York, bring keto snacks to munch on instead of sugary snacks

  o Make keto snacks ahead of time

This list has been broken down into bite-sized chunks. When you can do a task in one sitting, you're much more likely to complete it. In our example, this person can take ten minutes right away to set their alarm clock. Then, they can send a text message to Mindy, spend an hour or so researching recipes on Pinterest, and go to the library to pick up the books. On the way to the library, they can listen to Pandora radio and start gathering some songs to put on their workout playlist.

The psychology of using bite-sized tasks is incredible. When the tasks on your checklist are relatively simple, you'll be able to finish each task quicker. You feel good because you've made progress on your goals, and your brain is happy because you haven't lost sleep worrying about how you will complete the next step.

Again, I realize that this is a bit of a recap, as we already gone through building a checklist in chapter one and again in chapter two. However, to succeed, you must make sure that your checklist can provide a strong foundation for you as you follow your goals.

The Easiest Way to Take Steps

The easiest way for you to work toward your goal is to take one step at a time.

Right now, go ahead and do the *smallest* step on your checklist. Maybe your smallest step is to call someone, register for a class, or set your alarm clock. It doesn't have to be the *first* thing on your checklist; just the smallest or easiest task you can accomplish. Whatever your smallest step is, put this book down for a minute and take that step right now. This book can wait.

After You Complete Something on Your Checklist

All done with step one? Great job!

(If you didn't complete the step and kept reading ahead, you are a silly cheater! Go ahead and put this book down and complete something on that checklist of yours. This is your chance to get started on your goals, and you won't be able to reach your goals without the proper effort).

Now, take a minute and reflect on how easy it was to complete the first step. This is what it feels like to work on your goals. The smaller your steps are, the easier it will be to reach the final destination without exhausting yourself. You've already completed the first step on your checklist, so I will take this time to explain some of the struggles you might face in the future. Remember, you already have one success under your belt, which also means that you've already taken the first step.

Don't feel overwhelmed by the things that you might struggle with in the future; just remember that these are things that may or may not happen. You will be better equipped to deal with your struggles if you take some time to think about them before they happen.

Identifying Barriers: The Basics

Every goal has barriers, and it's impossible to have a goal without them unless your goal is to do something simple like sit on the couch for ten seconds (in which case, you may need to make some major life changes if your schedule won't allow you to sit down for ten seconds). Any goal that is worth fighting for will include a struggle of some kind. In this chapter, we will examine several common roadblocks that people face when trying to accomplish their goals, and I will let you in on some secrets to overcoming those struggles.

Every goal has its common barriers, roadblocks, and setbacks that you need to prepare yourself to face. Using some of the most common goals, let's take a look at the struggles that might come up and how you can conquer or avoid them.

Goals that involve becoming a better person can include things like becoming a better parent, spouse, and being nicer to others. Roadblocks that commonly affect these goals include:

- Children acting out, getting into fights with your spouse, other people cutting you off in traffic, cussing you out, and doing whatever they can to get your goat.

- Your own routine and personality. As time goes on, it becomes easy to settle into a routine and adopt past versions of yourself and your personality that you're more familiar with.

- Stress often impacts personality-related goals much stronger than other goals because when you're trying to improve your personality, your goal is ties directly to your emotional well-being. Of course, stress has a negative impact on your emotions.

You can overcome many of these struggles by shifting your focus back onto your goal multiple times throughout the day. The more times you recenter yourself and focus on your goals each day, the easier it will be to control yourself in these situations. Also, be sure to make time for self care and meditation to help lower your stress levels.

Goals that revolve around personal health and hygiene have different setbacks and struggles, including:

- Our natural, ingrained habit of procrastinating.

- A sugar or carbs addiction, in which the body continues to crave unhealthy foods and sometimes go through withdrawal symptoms like depression and fatigue.

- An instinct to avoid and dislike working out, until we finish a workout and feel the endorphins we release from doing exercise.

We can overcome these barriers pushing through and defeating procrastination, which we will be covering in the next two chapters. A strong accountability system is also essential for these goals in particular.

Goals like quitting an addiction are often known for their difficult struggles, which might include things like:

- The threat of relapse (which affects all goals, though it is most prominent in those that are addiction-related).

- Dealing with cravings, withdrawal symptoms, and finding ways to relieve or eliminate them.

- Admitting to others that you struggle with an addiction and asking for their help and support.

You can overcome these struggles by finding a good mentor and receiving advice from your doctor (please note that if your goal is to overcome an addiction, it is best to seek *professional help*. Addictions can be difficult to break, and you should not have to face an addiction by yourself. Therefore, if you struggle with an addiction, please seek professional help. Your future self will thank you).

Professional goals such as getting hired for a certain position or receiving a promotion have their own unique challenges, including:

- Meeting the minimum education requirements and years of experience for a position (especially if you're changing careers).

- Standing out from the competition in a good way.

- The challenges that surface if the job requires you to relocate, including housing, the cost of living in your new hometown, and moving expenses.

In a similar way, goals related to education (getting good grades, going back to school as an adult, or learning a new skill) pose challenges, including the following:

- Studying hard and applying yourself to the material.

- Financial concerns (for college students and those wanting to learn a new skill).

- Staying motivated when classes and courses become difficult.

We can overcome any of these challenges by beating procrastination and learning to schedule your time wisely.

These barriers are possible to overcome, but you need to think about these struggles ahead of time and plan out ways to push through them, so when the time comes, you'll know what to do.

You might also face some struggles that stem from your personality, including procrastination, working too hard and burning out, or anxiety about failing. We'll be cover procrastination in more detail in the next chapter. In the meantime, let's look at some of the struggles you might face within yourself.

Fear of Failure and Other Internal Barriers

"You're not good enough."

"You're not strong enough."

"You won't accomplish your goals because you failed in the past."

"You can't improve yourself."

"If you try again, you'll fail and everyone will laugh at you."

Do these words sound like something you may have heard in the past? Maybe these words came from inside your own head or from another person. These words come from our deeply rooted fear of failure.

One of the most common reasons that people quit working toward their goals is because they get in their own way. Many people have a hard time with overcoming their fears and anxiety about goal setting. They worry that they will fail, so they paralyze themselves and become too afraid to move forward.

We're all afraid of failure to some extent. Failure tells us that we aren't strong enough to change our circumstances, personalities or lives, so we should stop trying altogether. Unfortunately, most people deal with this fear of failure in the wrong way. Instead of facing and embracing their fear, these people decide to set no goals at all, even though they might be giving up their dreams by doing so.

To conquer this fear of failure, we need to realize that failure is not as bad as we make it sound. Let's say that my goal is to be more productive at work, and I don't meet my goals before the deadline. This is not a failure—this is just a sign that you need to adjust your goal and try again. Maybe your goal is too ambitious and you didn't give yourself enough time to finish it; next time, you need to adjust the deadline. You may even discover that you need to adjust the goal itself. You haven't failed, and you just need to readjust and try again.

Another component of the fear of failure is the fear that if you tell people about your goal, and then fail to achieve it, they will look down upon you as a failure. If you pick your accountability partners wisely, this will not happen. After you tell your friends and family about your goal, if you can't meet your goal by the deadline, ask for their advice. Tell them why your first plan isn't working and ask what they would do to adjust the goal. Your accountability partners are there to help you, and if you ask for their advice, they will give it to you. Don't just tell them, "Hey, I gave up trying to reach that goal because it was too hard." Engage them and ask, "Should I fix the deadline or try a new approach to reach this goal?"

The fear of failure is a natural instinct in the human brain, but it isn't healthy when you're trying to set and achieve your goals. The easiest way to overcome this fear is to think of failure in a new way. I recommend taking five minutes every day to think about how failure is not the end; it's just a sign that you should probably adjust something.

Don't let your fears dictate your success, as you are a completely capable person with the right to pursue your dreams.

We'll take a closer look at procrastination in the next few chapters, but for now, it's time to discuss how you can use your strengths to overcome barriers and procrastination in your goal setting.

Discovering Your Strengths

It's easier said than done. Finding your strengths on your own can be a difficult and even misleading task, but to overcome the struggles you will face in your goal setting, it's important to recognize your strengths and learn how to use them to build yourself up.

As I mentioned earlier, I was not an organized person before I got to college, and I had a terrible time struggling with procrastination. If I set a goal, I quickly lost interest because of all the steps I had to go through. However, when I took a closer look at my strengths and how I could use them to move past my procrastination problem, I was able to grow as a person and reap the benefits.

There are a lot of different ways to find and learn about your strengths. You could take an online test designed to find those strengths; however, these are normally inaccurate because studies have shown that most of us will overestimate our personal strengths and talents, such as kindness and generosity, which skews how the test is scored and thus, your results won't be accurate. Instead, the preferred method of discovering your strengths is to ask people who know you well and do some self-reflection on your own. I'll explain how to discover your strengths first, then we'll talk about how you can leverage your strengths to meet your goals.

Discovering your strengths can be tricky, especially when you dig beneath the superficial talents and try to uncover the way your heart works. It's not something we tend to think about on a normal basis, but once you find your strengths and name them, it becomes easier to see them in our daily lives. Imagine a young girl who hates how she has brown eyes, and she spends all day wishing she had blue eyes instead until her crush says, "Wow, your eyes are so cool!" Suddenly she sees her eyes in a new perspective, so she stops trying to hide her eyes and embraces herself for who she really is, all because one comment gave her a new perspective. When you hear other people describe your strengths, it opens your eyes to see the things you might not have thought of before.

To discover your strengths, the first and most important step is to ask the people you trust who also know you best, as the best way to get an accurate reflection of yourself is to have someone else hold the mirror. However, if you ask right off the bat what your greatest strengths are, you might get a lot of answers that focus on your hobby-related talents, such as "you're a great basketball player." Although those talents are a certain type of strength, they aren't the strengths that will help you meet your goals. So instead, try asking concrete questions, like "what is the best aspect of my character?" And when they tell you, ask, "Can you give me an example?" you can respond with, "What was a time when I was the most generous/thoughtful/proactive?"

Once you have asked somewhere between ten and twenty different people about what they consider to be your greatest strengths, go ahead and write down the answers you heard the most. Your list might look a little something like this:

- Open minded, creative, likes to come up with new ideas.

- Problem solving.

- Not worried to confront problems or difficult people head on.

Everyone's strengths are going to look different, and that is okay. Your strengths might not look amazing on paper, but don't worry—your strengths always look better in real life.

You can also learn about your strengths on your own, and one of the best ways to accomplish this is through brainstorming. Of course, this comes with the slippery slope of possible narcissistic thoughts and ideas, but if you're willing to be honest with yourself, it's not a bad idea to conduct a brainstorming session and list out what you believe to be your top strengths. Afterward, you can compare your personal list with the list of other people's responses, which can do worlds to help you in the next step of goal-setting success: how to identify the ways you can use your strengths to achieve your goals.

Using Your Strengths to Achieve Your Goals

Once you take the time to acknowledge your strengths, it's time to start channeling those strengths into your goal setting process and using your goals to overcome any barriers you might face. When you have an idea of your strengths in mind, the next step is to come up with a step-by-step response to your struggles and plan out some defense strategies.

For example, let's say that Shawn wants to get better at saving his money. He has brainstormed some possible barriers he might face, including his eating habits, his lack of understanding when it comes to saving money, and his tendency to make goals "in the moment" and not persevere in them. On the other hand, he surveys some of his closest friends and family, and they all say that Shawn is outgoing, understanding, and passionate. So, how can Shawn use his strengths to reach his goals?

One strategy he could employ is planning to depend on his passionate personality to help fuel his perseverance. If he can keep his excitement about saving money alive, he will have a healthy savings account set up in no time. Another possibility is that Shawn might need to take a step back and pause for some reflection. Does he truly understand himself? How would he treat the situation if it was happening to one of his best friends? His strengths can help him refocus his attention on the goal.

Shawn can also use his strengths to anticipate and redirect potential setbacks before they happen. He tends to spend a lot of money eating out with friends, which is not good for his goal of saving money. However, since Shawn is excellent at handling social situations, he can steer his friends away from eating out so often and get the group to try doing new things instead.

Annie wants to get better at self care and taking care of her needs. She will need to overcome a lot of bad habits, including her irregular sleep schedule, unhealthy eating habits, and her issues with negative body image. She has discovered that some of her strengths include working independently, problem solving, and organizing her time well.

One thing Annie might decide to do is use her strengths to make sure she sticks to a set schedule. This will utilize her goals of working independently and organizing her time. If this fails, she can rely on her problem solving strengths to figure out what went wrong and reorganize her schedule for another try.

On a deeper level, Annie can use her problem solving skills to answer tough questions about her goal when she wants to give up. She needs to be capable of being honest with herself, and then use that honesty to rework her plan.

It's easy to become discouraged if it seems like your strengths don't match up with your goal in any way. If this happens to you, don't despair; it's quite possible you just need a fresh perspective on the issue. Feel free to ask your mentor and accountability partners for their advice and opinions. No matter what your strengths are, you can use them to achieve your goals, though you might have to get a little creative.

Your Check-in Date Is...

So, you have a list (or at least a mental list) of all the potential barriers you might face and another a list of all your greatest strengths. You seem to be well on your way to figuring out how you can use these strengths to overcome your weaknesses, and you've even completed the first step towards achieving your goal. Great job!

Go ahead and take this time to complete the second smallest step on your goal checklist, if you haven't already. Then, we will go ahead and set up your check-in date.

Your **check-in date** will be a day halfway between your start date and the deadline for your goal. This will be the day that you take a look at your current progress and make sure that you are on track to achieve your goal by your deadline. You'll be sharing this date with your mentor and accountability partners, so try to make sure it's a date on which you will be available. If you can't meet with anyone face-to-face, at least try to leave yourself enough time to make a phone call with an accountability partner to go over your progress so far.

This date is almost as important as your primary deadline. As it is the halfway point, you will designate it as your chance to adjust what isn't working and improve your strategy. As explained, it is also a deadline in which you will be approximately halfway to your goal.

The most important thing to remember about this date is the progress that you want to make before this preliminary deadline. Even though I just said that your goal should be about 50%

complete by the first deadline, it's okay to bend that rule a little bit, especially if your goal is ongoing, such as the struggle to quit smoking or strengthen a relationship. While you're busy picking a date for this check-in day, jot down some ideas about where you would like to be by this date. How close to success do you want to be? Where can you envision yourself being at this point? It's okay if you don't believe you'll be halfway to meeting your goals by this date. Some goals are more of a process, and the official deadline you choose for yourself might be for one aspect of your goal.

Once you select a date for your check-in deadline and brainstorm what you want your progress to look like before that deadline, it's a good idea to set yourself some reminders over the next few days, weeks, or months. I recommend setting reminders and alarms on your phone to remind you about the steps you need to take. Some example reminders you might use include things like, "Smile at coworkers today," "Call my therapist," "Hug Lily," and "Go to the gym tomorrow." Short, sweet, and to the point.

After setting up some reminders, it is then time to tell your mentor and accountability partners about your new check-in date. They don't need to meet with you in person, but if they could take some time to talk about your progress with you and give their advice, let them know that their time would be greatly appreciated.

Get to Work on that Checklist!

Now is the time. You've planned your goals, selected one or more of them to work on, and brainstormed some different ways to tackle those goals. You discovered some interesting ideas to work with your unique style of planning your time and created a step-by-step guide to formulating your action plan. You have rallied together a support system of accountability partners, and you sought out one or more people to ask for their mentorship. You even took some time to identify potential barriers you could face in the future and used your personal strengths to overcome those.

Once you have completed all these steps, you will finally be on the road to success. You can reach your goals, and you will be successful in whatever you choose to apply yourself. However, to reach that point of success, you need to do one more thing…

It's impossible to reach your goals without work. To reach that success and that moment when you achieve your goals and where you can raise your fists in the air and give a loud, triumphant shout will all come, so long as you work hard for it. As you continue through the rest of this book, keep crossing items off your checklist. You will reach this goal, and you will not let yourself fail. Stick with the subgoals and steps that you brainstormed for yourself, and you'll make it to the end of the tunnel.

Don't stop focusing on your goal. Hard work starts now.

Chapter Four:
Defeating Procrastination

Coming from a family of chronic procrastinators, it's pretty safe to say that procrastination has been one of the biggest personal struggles I have dealt with in the past. At one point, it grew to be so overwhelming that I eventually worried it would hold me back from pursuing my dreams.

No matter what your goals are, procrastination is an issue you will need to overcome. According to studies published in *Psychological Science,* procrastination might be a genetic trait. If your parents and grandparents were procrastinators, you will probably struggle with procrastination as well. Unfortunately, in addition to being a genetic trait, procrastinating is also often a lifelong trait.

This doesn't mean that you can't overcome your procrastination habits (thank goodness!), but you could never reach a point in your life where you no longer procrastinate. If LaKeisha procrastinates about her chores all throughout elementary school, middle school, and high school, her habits won't change once she enters college. If she does nothing to reverse her procrastination habits, it won't stop when she turns forty, and it still won't stop when she turns ninety. Unless LaKeisha decides to turn her life around and stop procrastinating, her habits won't stop on their own. Her procrastination will become a lifelong trait.

Since I was a chronic procrastinator in the past, I understand that procrastination is a difficult habit to break, especially because breaking it requires fighting against your own habits and instincts. It feels like the mountain is too big to move, so why keep trying to change yourself? You'll just fall back into procrastination again.

In this chapter, I will share some strategies you can use to overcome procrastination and stop saying, "I'll do it tomorrow." As someone who struggled with procrastination for most of my life, I can safely say that several of these tactics and ideas have worked for me in the past, and I'm excited to share them with you, so you can fight back against the urge to procrastinate. It may take a few tries before you get the hang of it, but with a little bit of hard work, you can push through to the other side and reach a point where you can be productive without saying, "I'll do it tomorrow."

Before We Get Started

Let's take a quick pause and discuss some important points about procrastination and your productivity. The following are some things that you should know before we move forward.

First of all, everyone has moments of procrastination. Procrastination is often genetic, meaning that people who are born into families of procrastinators are more likely to procrastinate than the average person, but everyone procrastinates from time to time, regardless of their genetic makeup. It's part of human nature to want free time and work on our own terms, and for most of us, if we had things our way, we wouldn't have to work at all. This is why when parents raise their children without responsibilities, the children are more likely to have a hard time adjusting to life as adults. If we didn't need to work, we won't, unless we have a good reason to do it. So don't feel bad about the occasional "I'll get it done later," because we've all done it before. It's only when procrastination becomes a habit that you should take serious steps to remove it from your life.

Secondly, procrastination is not something to be ashamed of. Don't be afraid to admit it to your accountability partners, your friends, and your mentor, and ask for their advice on how to conquer the urge to procrastinate. Your habits aren't a cause for shame, which applies even if you've conquered procrastination and then relapsed several times in a row. Procrastination is something that you must fix, not something you should hide, and fixing it will be a long process that will take time.

I want to take a moment to recognize if maybe one of your goals is to procrastinate less. That's great! It's a worthwhile goal that will help you in all other areas of your life. However, for the purpose of this chapter, I will assume that you have a different goal that you're busy working on, and you're looking for some tips and pointers to help you stop procrastinating, so you can be more productive and achieve your goals.

Five Reasons You Need to Stop Procrastinating

It's the truth—we all want to be successful in life. Very few people sit around on the couch and say to themselves, "I want to be a failure." The human race is constantly improving. We dream about the future, we invent new things and ideas, we learn more about ourselves and our surroundings every day, and we put a lot of value on improving ourselves, both as individuals and as a society. All of us are always striving to do and be better.

At this point in history, the only thing that keeps us from setting goals and achieving them is procrastination.

The first step in defeating procrastination is realizing there is a problem. We will take a few minutes to walk through five reasons why you should stop procrastinating. To change your procrastination habits, you need to believe that you will be better off without them. So, here are my top five reasons for why you need to stop procrastinating.

1. **Your stress levels and mental health**—Stress increases when you put off a task until the last minute, and the constant, extra stress that accompanies this action can take a heavy toll on your mental health and overall wellbeing.

2. **Your personal health and safety**—In some cases, by procrastinating, you can create an unhealthy or even dangerous situation for yourself. For example, by putting off replacing a leak in the roof, mold will probably on the ceiling, and you putting off cleaning the mold until you

begin sneezing and coughing from having been breathing it in for so long can lead to terrible outcomes. If untreated, you could develop serious health issues from the mold. Although this may seem like an extreme example, it is what could happen without some productivity plan in place.

3. **Your relationships with your family and friends**—Who enjoys being around a friend that says things like, "I'll pay you back next week" every week? Family members can never convince you to be productive, and they wonder if you will ever do well in your career. Your family and friends will likely lose their trust in you because you keep promising that you'll finish whatever needs to happen, but as the weeks pass, you still have yet to do it.

4. **Your life right now**—You don't want to have these things hanging over your head all week, do you? Sure, it seems easier to put off the hard work until tomorrow, but why put that extra stress on your subconscious? You will feel better if you can

complete what you have on your plate earlier rather than later.

5. **Your future**—You owe this to your future self. You should be able to look back and thank yourself for being productive with the tasks you needed to complete and making your life easier. For example, if your goal was to save for retirement, but you keep putting it off until tomorrow, what will your future self think when you've pushed back retirement another five years because you didn't start saving soon enough?

As you work on your goals, remember that procrastination will stop your progress unless you do something about it. You owe this to yourself, your future, and everyone around you. It's time to stop saying, "I'll get to it tomorrow."

Let's go ahead and dive in to some proven strategies to help you overcome procrastination and stay on track with being productive and reaching your goals.

Identify Procrastination Triggers

According to research conducted by Dr. Timothy Pychyl, everyone has reasons why they procrastinate on tasks. The task might be boring, difficult, unstructured, ambiguous, frustrating, not rewarding enough, or lacking in personal meaning, and any combination of these factors can lead to procrastination. However, if you can figure out how to reverse these procrastination triggers, it can reduce your procrastination drastically.

I will explain a couple of examples of how to do this. Let's say that Vihaan has to write his senior thesis, and he can't seem to stop procrastinating about it. When he takes a closer look at the issue, he discovers that he doesn't want to work on the project because it's boring. To reverse this trigger, Vihaan decides to turn the project into a competition and contacts his friends who are also working on their thesis papers. The person to write the most words in thirty minutes wins.

Wendy is also struggling with procrastination. She wants to eat healthier, but every day, it becomes so much easier to go through the drive-thru than it is to go home and cook vegetables for herself. However, when she stops to examine why she's procrastinating so much, it turns out that she's not struggling with the difficulty, but with a lack of reward, as she doesn't see any reward in going home to eat healthy food. Therefore, to reverse this trigger, she takes some time to find some low sugar dessert recipes, and she bakes them ahead of time and keeps them on the kitchen counter. After she's eaten a full, healthy meal, she rewards herself with a low sugar blueberry scone.

As you make progress towards your goal, what are some of the reasons you procrastinate? Is the task boring, frustrating, and difficult? Or does it lack personal meaning? Once you have identified the root cause of your procrastination, you can brainstorm some ways to reverse the procrastination triggers and be productive again. You may need to do this multiple times for one goal, which is totally normal. Maybe it starts off boring, so you add new aspects to make it interesting. Then, six days later, you start procrastinating again because the project isn't rewarding enough. Be ready to make continuous adjustments, so you can continue defeating procrastination.

Over the last few years, I have discovered something that has helped redefine how I view goal setting: as long as I keep moving forward, I will get to my destination. It's like taking a road trip across the country; you have somewhere to go, but if you stop and spend the night in every hotel along the way, you won't get to your destination, and you will spend all summer sleeping in hotels and telling yourself, "We won't stop so soon tomorrow. Tomorrow we'll drive the rest of the way." To get to your destination, you need to get back in the car and drive; so long as you keep driving in the right direction and minimize the number of stops you make, you'll get there eventually.

Procrastination wants you to stop at every point along the way, but you've got to identify the triggers, overcome them, and keep moving forward.

The Five Minute Miracle

Over time, scientific studies have discovered that one of the best ways to break out of procrastination is to try the **Five Minute Miracle** method. Isaac Newton's law of inertia states that an object put into motion will stay in motion until an outside force stops it. Of course, he was talking about objects that physically move, but the same basic principle applies to our brains and how we think. In the 1920s, psychologist Bluma Zeigarnik discovered that when people start working on a task, but a force interrupts them before they can finish, they will continue thinking about that task; however, if people complete a bunch of different tasks at the same time, they are much less likely to remember anything they completed.

Let's look at a quick example of this phenomenon. Yolanda and Danielle are both waitresses at a local restaurant. Yolanda serves five tables, completing every order. Then, she has a twenty minute break, and her manager asks her, "What did table 16 order?" Chances are, Yolanda won't be able to remember. On the other hand, Danielle is continuously serving tables, and she never has a break in between customers. She still has four unfinished orders when her manager asks her, "What did table 16 order?" Since Danielle's brain is still busy working on her unfinished tasks, she is much more likely to remember that table 16 ordered three cheeseburgers.

This is one of the reasons why cliffhangers in books and TV shows work so well. If everything wraps up too perfectly, our brains consider the case closed and stop thinking about it. On the other hand, if a character is in danger, we can't stop thinking about it because our brain senses unfinished business in the story.

You can use this psychology trick to your advantage. Once you force your brain to work on a task, if you leave some of the task unfinished, your brain will continue to work on that task after you stop. To use this tool, set a timer for five minutes and do nothing except work on your goal for those five minutes. Don't complete everything, as it's important to leave your brain on a cliffhanger. As soon as your five minutes is up, stop working and take a break. Repeat as needed until you can work comfortably for twenty minutes at a time.

Getting in the Mood to Work

While we're trying to defeat procrastination, it's easy to focus on the procrastinating part while forgetting about how we also have to be productive. There are lots of resources out there for increasing your productivity, though here, we will simply touch on a few of the basics.

When you have a lot of work to get done, sometimes the most helpful thing you can do for yourself is to get yourself in the right mood. Maybe your desk is a mess, or you're working in a noisy area with lots of people talking around you, or you aren't doing enough to keep your brain awake. I'm going to discuss some of the ways you can optimize your workspace for productivity using just a few simple steps.

The first step is to address the color. Depending on where you are, you might not be able to do anything about this aspect, but in most cases, you can use color choices to improve your productivity. According to numerous studies, blue has been linked to higher productivity, though color psychologist Angela Wright believes that blue is not for everyone. Blue is best for people who do a lot of "mind work," such as accountants. For people who need to be creative, a bright yellow may link better with productivity. And if you're looking for more of a balanced, natural feel, go with a soft green color to refresh and balance the mind.

You may be in a position to paint the walls of your office space if you work from home. However, in the case that you don't have an office space or if your work space belongs to a company, try using color in unexpected ways. You can use color-themed office supplies, such as blue pencil holders, blue post-it notes, a blue stapler, and blue paper clips. You can also add small objects to decorate your space, such as yellow picture frames and a sunflower wall calendar.

What if your goal is something along the lines of personal improvement and not a career-related goal? Try giving your desk a color makeover anyway. You might find your productivity improve, and if not, at least your space is organized and decorated, which will still help eliminate stress.

After improving the color situation in your workspace, the next step is to try improving the music playlists you use in your routine. Music that contains lyrics is actually not that great to play in the background when you're working because the lyrics can distract the part of your brain that processes human speech. To reach full productivity, try looking up study music on Spotify, YouTube, or any other streaming service you can listen to music on. The best music for studying is soft instrumental music that isn't too catchy and is easy for your brain to tune out as you work. If the tune is too catchy, you might find yourself focusing on the song and not on your work. There are a lot of high quality study music playlists out there that you can listen to for free, so you should try giving some of them a shot.

Perhaps you don't work in an office; maybe you work as a freelancer, or you're currently in the middle of a job search and your favorite place to get work done is either the library or your local coffee shop. These can definitely be great places to finish your work, but if you're trying to be productive in a place that has lots of people, it might be an even better idea to invest in some noise cancelling headphones. These can work wonders for your productivity if you work in a crowded place in which many people are talking.

Blocking Websites and Other Productivity Hacks

One productivity hack you might try is to install a website blocking app on your phone or computer. These apps and extensions are designed to help you focus when you're supposed to be working, and when activated, they block the sites that you enter on your "block list." Some apps will block the websites on a schedule that you select (such as from 2 PM to 5 PM on Fridays). Other apps will wait for you to turn on the blocking feature, and all the distracting websites will remain blocked until you finish your work. Sometimes, apps will even have a "whitelist" setting, in which you can enter one or two websites that the app won't block, while it blocks all other websites. These apps and web extensions can be productivity saviors, especially if your goal involves working online for any length of time.

Another idea is to use timers, as we briefly discussed with the Five Minute Miracle. When you use a timer to stay focused on a task, you will be more likely to finish what you're working on in less time. You will also protect yourself from burnout. To get started, pick the simplest timer you can find, preferably one that is not connected to your smartphone, and set it for twenty minutes. Try to get as much work done as you can before the timer rings, then set the timer for five minutes and take a stretch break. You can use the timer to turn your goal into a race while making sure that you don't stop working before your time's up and keeping your five-minute break from becoming a five-hour siesta. You can find a dependable egg timer for as little as $5.

If you believe your pace is too fast and you can't keep up with the items you put on your to-do list, it's okay to slow down, as long as you're still being productive. Sometimes, we give ourselves too much work and not enough time to complete it. Unless your deadline is from an outside source, it's okay to slow down a little bit and focus on one thing at the time. You can try for two days not worrying about the deadline. Set a specific time for working on your goal, then work on something else. Your brain might need to hit the refresh button, which you can do by giving yourself a chance to slow down. When you're ready, you can return to your normal pace.

And of course, don't forget the best productivity hack for today's technological society: turn off your phone!

When Nothing Else Works: Kicking Yourself in the Pants

There will be times when nothing seems to work. You identified the triggers, used the Five Minute Miracle, blocked all your social media sites while you work, and used timers to try and stay on track. Still however, you keep putting it off until tomorrow.

In certain cases, you won't have the luxury of waiting until tomorrow, and other times, you might just need to give yourself a nudge in the right direction or even a good kick in the pants. You need to get yourself moving again! Now is the time to get started on improving yourself and your life. If you do nothing, nothing will get better.

When you're struggling with procrastination, you need to shift your focus and lean on one of two things: either the *pain* or the *reward*.

Focusing on the pain is your **kick in the pants** or your "get it done or else" moment of absolute honesty. When you're trying to eat healthy, your kick in the pants moment might be watching a documentary on diabetes. If you don't eat healthy, you could potentially develop diabetes. When you're trying to manage your finances, take a moment to realize exactly how bad it would be to go broke. When you're trying to fix a relationship, imagine the unimaginable happening.

Once you've taken the time to focus on what you could lose, reshift your focus to the rewards you could reap. Not just the reward that you set up for yourself (although it's good to remind yourself of that from time to time), but the rewards that come from completing your goal, whether it's more energy, a healthy bank account, or a happy and fulfilling marriage. What are some of the best rewards from completing your goal? In five years, if someone asks how you've changed, what would you say to them? Close your eyes and do your best to imagine the day when you have reached your goal. When that day comes, you will be so proud of yourself. All this work will be completely worth it.

Now, keeping the pain and the reward in mind, grab your timer and do another Five Minute Miracle. You can do this. I believe in you, because I used to procrastinate all the time, and now I can meet my goals. If I can make it, so can you.

A Final Note About Procrastination

Procrastination is a tough habit to break, but you can definitely break it. It may take a few tries, and that's okay. Just remember that if you can be productive right now, you won't have to worry about pushing it back to tomorrow to get it done.

Hopefully, your goal checklist is progressing well. If not, go ahead and put this book down for a bit and take some time to work on that checklist. Don't worry if you've procrastinated and now you're behind where you wanted to be at this point. Again, right now, you can still change that procrastination and become productive.

Chapter Five:
Staying Focused When Life Happens

Sometimes, life gets in the way of our goals, and despite our best intentions, we find ourselves putting our goals aside to survive whatever life is throwing at us. This could be anything from an inconvenient project at work to a full-scale emergency. While most of us hopefully won't experience any emergencies during the next few weeks, none of us can predict our futures, and we don't know for certain what tomorrow has in store for us; therefore, it's always important to come prepared.

What happens if you fall and break your leg tomorrow, and you can't keep up with your exercise plan for the next two months? Or, what if you're making great progress towards your dream job, but your elderly parent suffers from a heart attack, and you need to put down your goals to take care of your ailing parent?

In this chapter, we will cover some of the ways in which you can stay focused on your goals when life tries to get in your way, whether those inconveniences are small blunders or critical emergencies. Your goals will require perseverance, which you build and strengthen when you overcome obstacles. Let's get started on this topic by looking at the history of the word *perseverance*.

The Meaning of Perseverance

Perseverance is a word straight out of the latin language. In Latin, we can break down the word *perseverance* into the smaller prefix "per" (meaning *thoroughly*) and the derivative suffix "severus" (meaning *severe*), so *perseverus* means that something is very strict. The Latin word "perseverare" means to abide by something strictly. In all forms of the word, *strictness* is involved somehow.

This offers a lot of insight to the meaning behind perseverance. Our modern dictionary defines **perseverance** as persistence in doing something, even if it's difficult to continue. The difficulties are severe, but the person has enough strength and stamina to push through to the other side.

In many cases, there is a difference between *perseverance* and *stubbornness*. Let's say that Xavier wants to become a YouTube star, but YouTube, for whatever reason, demonetized his videos and he has no followers. He could persevere and fix his videos so they can be monetized again, and then tell all his friends to subscribe to his channel. Or he could be stubborn and leave his videos the way they are, saying, "Well, if I just keep going, it'll get better soon." Perseverance includes knowing when you need to reevaluate, but also pushing through the rough times.

With this definition in mind, let's look at some of the psychology behind perseverance and how it applies to goal setting.

How You Can Use the Psychology of Perseverance to Enjoy Goal Setting

According to many psychologists, perseverance is only interesting or worthwhile when the brain releases **dopamine**. If the brain does not release dopamine, you won't enjoy doing the tasks that require perseverance. To train your brain to persevere, it's important to keep the dopamine levels in your brain high.

The brain contains its own reward system that it uses to control the sensations of pleasure, accomplishment, and happiness. This reward system is nothing more than a hormone called dopamine, and yet it's one of the most powerful tools that you can harness in your goal setting pursuits. Without using dopamine, perseverance becomes almost impossible.

I'm not saying that you should depend on harmful habits like substance abuse to get a dopamine rush. You must train your brain to enjoy perseverance, which you can do using several different tricks, some of which we have already completed. The following sections outline my top five strategies to increase dopamine release when working on perseverance.

1. Willpower is not as strong as pleasure, so focus on changing your mindset. Psych yourself up before working on your goals, as doing so will affect your overall performance. Tell yourself how fun this work is and how much you will love completing the items on your goal checklist. If you trick your brain into getting excited about the work, you will be more likely to enjoy hard work in the future.

2. Break down your goals into the tiniest subgoals possible. If your goal takes more than ten minutes to complete, break it down even further. This method can help increase the amount of dopamine your brain releases while you work. Your brain will feel a lot more accomplished if you complete five much smaller tasks instead of one large task. We discussed this step in the earlier

chapters, and now you know exactly why we did that—you're teaching your brain to enjoy working on goals!

3. If you can, turn your simple, goal-related tasks into puzzles. How can I organize my afternoon to fit in all these activities? How can I clean the house and work on my goals at the same time? The human brain is built to love puzzles and riddles, and when you figure out the answer, your brain releases dopamine to congratulate itself. As long as you can figure out the answer to the puzzle, this strategy can be an effective tactic to release more dopamine while you persevere.

4. Engage in light exercise while thinking about your goals. A brisk power walk coupled with planning your career goals is a great way to connect the endorphins from exercising with the dopamine from solving goal-related problems. Plus, you get a chance to kill two birds with one stone and keep yourself healthy at the same time (however, it's best to stick with light exercise, whatever that means for you and your current level of fitness. You want to be able to focus your

mind on your goals and not on the fact that you're out of breath).

5. Accomplish something every day and celebrate it! If we don't accomplish at least one thing every day, we quickly become apathetic and unmotivated, which can lead to depression over time. By completing at least one task every day and taking a few moments to feel good about it, you are giving your brain a chance to release dopamine in relation to your goals and your perseverance. After a while, your brain will want to be more productive because you have trained it to enjoy hard work.

Teaching your brain to enjoy perseverance is a long and gradual process. You can start the learning process today, whether or not you are in a situation that requires it.

Perseverance and Self Care

In addition to refocusing the brain to enjoy perseverance, it's important to remember some of the basics of self care too at this point in the process. Whether your life is moving at the same pace it always has, or if you find yourself in the midst of an emergency and feel you're ready to give up on all your goals, one of the most important things you can do to stay grounded is to take care of yourself. Without self care, you will become discouraged and give up on your goals when all you really needed was some quality time by yourself.

First, take a shower, bath, or bubble bath just for the fun of it. Use your favorite body wash and throw in a bath bomb for some added fragrance or some epsom salts to help relax any sore muscles. When you're done, put on a cleansing face mask and take five minutes to close your eyes and relax. Put in earplugs if you have to and delegate work to other family members; whatever it takes, you need these five minutes.

Feeling better? Now, for your next meal, eat at least two different types of vegetables, one serving of healthy protein, and a tall glass of water. By skipping grains, caffeine, and sugar for one meal, you keep your brain clear so you can feel healthier and think clearer. You should also make sure you keep exercising.

To keep working toward your goals, you need perseverance, and to grow perseverance, you must take good care of yourself mentally and physically. To take care of your spiritual health, I recommend connecting with other members of your religious organization or reconnecting with yourself through yoga and meditation.

When It's Time to Say Enough is Enough

Let's say that Victoria wants to start her own business selling custom pet portraits. However, she has two backdrops, one prop, and her only camera is from 2002, meaning it's quite outdated. She has only taken two pet portraits in two months, and she's nowhere near her goal of ten customers per week. So, she decides that to persevere, she will have to double her marketing efforts and lower her prices to attract more customers. Unfortunately, instead of attracting more customers, she ends up earning even less than before.

At the end of high school, Braden wants to go to college and graduate with $0 in student loans. He can't pay for his college tuition and didn't get enough scholarship money through financial aid, so his parents agree to pay his way through college. Right before he goes away to college, Braden's mom suffers from a life-threatening brain tumor, and the surgery to remove it is so expensive it destroys the family's finances. Even though Braden is glad that his mom got the surgery she needed, he can no longer afford to go to college. Does he take on the mountains of student loans, or does he stay home and get a job flipping burgers for the next few months?

Alyssa wants to be a social media celebrity with over 100,000 followers, but even though she follows all the tips and tricks, she has barely gotten 200 followers. She finds a website promising her to get her 500,000 followers for just $50, and she has the money. However, is this the way to reach her goals? Maybe her account just needs that extra boost, and then it will get easier to get 100,000 followers on top of the 500,000 purchased followers.

Sometimes, it's okay to stop pushing forward with your goals. There are lots of cases where pushing ahead with a goal or idea could actually get you in more trouble than just stopping or changing your strategy. For now, we will focus on the cases in which you would need to take a break from your goal or even put it aside altogether.

Always remember that you should never give up on the goal setting. Even though there are circumstances in which you should put a certain goal to one side, you shouldn't give up on your dreams completely. Find new goals and work toward achieving those instead. With that in mind, here are some reasons why you might need to put your goal down for a while and reevaluate whether you want to continue moving forward.

- **You don't see this as a goal to work toward anymore**. Perhaps, two months ago, you dreamed of working in a certain position, but you have new information or a fresh outlook, and you no longer want that job. If you dread the moment when you achieve your goal, it is a clear sign that your current goal is not a good one to have, and you might want to reevaluate why you're pursuing it and if it would be a better idea to stop.

- **Your goal is having a negative impact on your health, your family, or your wallet.** You shouldn't give up at the first sign of difficulty, but if any of these three things are causing you too much negative stress, try pausing your goal for a week or two. After taking a break, you can decide if you should continue, refocus your goals, or simply stop working on this goal and start something different. This is the advice that Victoria in our example needs to follow. After taking a break from her business, she can rethink her goal.

- **The process to reach your goal includes doing something that violates your values.** For example, in the case of Alyssa buying social media followers, she needs to find new ways to reach her goal or reevaluate whether her goal is actually good for her to achieve. If you have to go against your values to complete a goal, it's probably best to move on.

What about Braden, the kid who wanted to become an engineer?

Braden still wants to be an engineer, but he also still wants to stay out of debt. He hasn't changed his goals, but setbacks in his life caused roadblocks in his original plan. Should he put his goals aside at this point? Absolutely not! His case is a situation in which fate has messed up a few steps of the goal, but the goal *itself* is not bad and Braden has not lost his motivation. In this case, Braden needs to come up with a new set of steps and subgoals to reach his ultimate goal. Perhaps he could start by finding a part time job and deciding to sell his airpods. He could then contact the college financial aid office and update them on his situation, asking what other scholarships might be available. He could decide to take a break from working on his goal, but he definitely should not give up just yet; he needs to stick with his goals and build his perseverance skills.

So, how do you tell when you're just procrastinating or when you genuinely need to change your strategy? The best way to tell the difference between procrastination and a problem that you need to fix is by asking yourself, "What's stopping me from taking this one step in particular?" If one of the steps on

Braden's goal checklist is to contact the financial aid office at his future college, and the reason he can't do that is because he's tired, it's *procrastination*. If he can't contact financial aid because he's at work during office hours, that's a problem that he should take steps to *fix*, either by making a phone call during his lunch break or by sending an email instead.

Also, you might need to ask yourself the question, "Is my goal actually realistic?" In a case that it isn't realistic, it's a good idea to go back to chapter one of this book and figure out if your goal is a good one to pursue. You can always change your goal later if it isn't realistic for you and your situation, and one example of this could be any goal that goes against your genetic makeup.

Dealing With Emergencies

Emergencies can include, but are not limited to: sickness, injury, mental health struggles, an ailing friend or family member, a fire, or a natural disaster, and it can happen to any of us at one time or another. We all have to deal with emergency situations at some point in our lives, and emergencies rarely happen at a convenient time. When an emergency does happen, it's far too easy to stop everything in our lives and focus all our energy on handling the mess in front of us, while letting our goals slip out of sight.

How you deal with an emergency situation and continue working on your goals at the same time is completely different from one person to the next. I will use two different examples to illustrate ways that you can persevere in your life.

Megan is a mother of four children, and her goal is to get out of debt and build up her savings account. However, in the middle of her crazy life with a full time job, parenting her children, and caring for her father, there is an accident, and her youngest son Oliver is bleeding and has to go to the hospital. She drops off the older kids at the house and rushes to get Oliver to the hospital, but on the way, her car gets a flat tire. After changing the tire, she gets Oliver to the hospital, only to discover that he is going to need stitches. Both the stitches and the new tire cost a lot of money—money that Megan was planning to put toward paying the mortgage.

There are a few different things Megan could do in this situation, but the first on her priority list should be Oliver. No matter the cost, people and health should always come first. Megan should never ignore Oliver's injuries so she could pay the mortgage. Also, she should fix the car tire because she will need that vehicle to get to work every day. Therefore, both of these costs are non-negotiable.

In this scenario, Megan should do the following:

- **Stay as calm and positive as possible**. In the example, we can assume that Megan felt like crying at first when she heard how expensive the tire and the stitches would be, but she told herself, "At least Oliver will be okay, and at least the rest of my children are also okay. At least I have medical insurance, and the tire didn't cause my car to wreck." Staying calm not only helps the current situation, but also keeps your mind clear for the next step.

- **Evaluate the situation**. Megan is stressed about the money, but at least she knows that the tire and the stitches won't be recurring expenses, so she can take care of the emergency now, then focus on her goals afterwards. When she's done dealing with Oliver's injury and the flat tire, she can focus on ways to earn back the money she spent.

- **Adjust her plan accordingly**. Megan decides to ask for a raise at work, and she takes some time to look up side gigs and ways to earn money online. She also decides that she can't afford to buy coffee every morning, so she switches to drinking the free coffee at her work.

Now, let's take a look at Jack. Jack is making progress in his effort to lose weight, and he's stuck with the exercise plan that his doctor recommended. He lives alone in his apartment, and his parents live across the country. One day, when Jack finishes working out, he gets an intense headache, and it gets so bad he ends up calling an ambulance. Turns out, he had a brain aneurysm (a bulging blood vessel in the brain that could potentially become deadly), and it will require surgery. The surgery is obviously non-negotiable, so how does Jack handle this situation?

Once again, people come first; therefore, Jack needs to follow the doctor's orders as far as resting and staying in bed. He will also be eating hospital food during his stay for surgeries, tests, and other medical procedures, despite how the hospital food will probably have a negative effect on his weight loss goals, as it doesn't fit into Jack's diet plan. However, even though the circumstances negatively affected his goal, Jack's life should come first.

In this situation, Jack needs to:

- **Stay as calm and positive as possible**. In his case, staying well-rested could very well mean the difference between life and death because it is not a good idea to ignore Jack's brain aneurysm. His doctor will have advice for Jack on how to stay calm.

- **Evaluate the situation**. Jack will have to go through brain surgery, which often has an extensive recovery period, so he won't be working out or following his diet plan during his stay at the hospital.

- **Adjust his plan accordingly**. While he's in the hospital, there isn't much Jack can do besides watch the portion size of the food he eats. He can also discuss his exercise plan with his doctor and see if he should change his exercise plan after the surgery. After his hospital stay, he can go back to his weight loss goals if the doctor says it's okay for him to do so.

Switching gears, let's take a look at an example of an emergency caused by a natural disaster.

Wayne wants to become more productive at his job and his everyday life. He is doing well in his career and personal life until one day, out of the blue, an earthquake hits and cracks the walls of his house in multiple places. As a result of the earthquake, one of the pipes in his bathroom bursts, and a gas leak under the house sets it on fire. Wayne manages to escape the flames, but his home is completely destroyed, and he has to start from square one.

Can you guess the steps that Wayne should follow to move forward from this emergency?

When you are faced with an emergency, the best way to handle yourself and your goals is to follow the steps we covered with Megan and Jack. People always come first, so Wayne should make sure that everyone is safe and taken care of before doing anything else. He is fine, and we can assume that everyone else in the house is fine too. After that, Wayne should stay calm and positive to keep himself from overstressing. Losing a house is quite a stressful situation, both financially and emotionally, and he lost all of his belongings in the fire too; therefore, he has nothing except for the clothes on his back and the phone in his pocket. It's probably a good idea for Wayne to take a couple of days off from pursuing his goals and focus on the situation at hand.

Next, Wayne should evaluate the situation, looking for how the disaster affected his goals and what he can do to fix the setbacks; after that, he can finally adjust his plan accordingly. Of course, depending on your situation, it may be best for you to change your strategy, or you may need to put down your goals and take a break.

After most emergencies, it can be difficult to pick up the pieces from where you left off before the incident. When your brain spends so much energy focusing on stressful events, you can quickly lose focus on your goals and for good reason. However, once you stop thinking about your goals, it's easy to believe that you also failed. Many people experience this feeling of failure, which is common among people who set New Year's resolutions; therefore, we will discuss this situation a bit more and discover why it may not always be such a bad thing to fail.

What if I Fail to Reach My Goals?

All of us have experienced failure at some point in our lives, unless your name is Clark Kent and you are secretly Superman. It's part of being a human, and when we set goals for ourselves, we are almost guaranteed to feel like a failure at least once during the process. However, it's important for us to remember that there is no such thing as completely failing your goals.

Yes, you read that correctly: there is no such thing as completely failing your goals. Let me explain; for most of us, the failure to reach a goal is a sign that we've reached the end of the road, in which we gain back the pounds we lost, we don't get the job, or our relationships fall apart despite our best intentions. At this point, it's common to put the goal down and say, "Well, it isn't meant to be," and move forward with our lives, leaving the goal behind.

If you have struggled with goal setting in the past, this situation might be a common refrain in your life. You've started so many goals and new year's resolutions that you've lost count of how many times you've said, "This time, it will be different." Every time you miss your expectations, you feel what some call the *guilt of failure*.

Today, I am here to tell you that you cannot fail to meet your goals; you simply put them down because you're not ready to complete them yet.

Maybe, you're not ready on an emotional level to meet this goal. You still have growing to do, which may or may not appear obvious to you right now. Perhaps, your physical health might need to improve before you set out towards your goals. If you can't run a mile today, you probably can't run a marathon tomorrow. Even giving yourself a week to train won't be enough, and that's okay. Sometimes, your goal is good to have, but you aren't quite ready for it, and you might need to wait another six months before picking it up and giving it another shot.

There is no such thing as a complete failure in the world of goal setting. If you can't meet your goals, it might be for one of four reasons:

- **Your goal is too difficult for your current physical or mental state**. It's possible to have the right goal at the wrong time. Again, especially if your goal is something physical like losing weight, don't feel discouraged if your goal is too difficult to handle right away. You might need to reevaluate whether your goal is realistic, or if you're just going through a procrastination phase.

- **You feel like you can't move forward because your life contains lots of outside stress and you're coming close to burnout**. This situation is when it becomes vital to take a break from your goals and focus on taking care of yourself. There's no shame in putting down a goal that is causing too much strain on your mind, body, or wallet; from there, you can decide whether you should pick it up and pursue it again.

- **You encounter an emergency that prevents you from moving forward with your goals**. As we just discussed with Braden, Megan, and Wayne, you can work through emergencies while making sure you also take care of yourself. Allow yourself time to pursue your goals when you're ready, and reevaluate your direction if applicable to the situation.

- **You could also just be struggling with procrastination**. In this case, go back and revisit chapter four, where we discussed how to deal with procrastination and some proven tricks to get your productivity back on track.

It's impossible to fail at a goal; you just decide to put it down for a while.

How to Restart an Old Goal

When you believe it's time to revisit an old goal, you will want to make sure you do the following steps:

- **Make sure you're now in a better place that you were before physically and emotionally to pursue the goal.** How have you grown since you stopped working on that goal? Are you ready to fix any problems that came up in the past? Are you better prepared this time?

- **Reevaluate the subgoals and steps you'll want to take.** Is your checklist realistic? Can you expect to finish this goal by completing these steps?

- **Don't feel shame or guilt for not having completed this goal in the past.** For whatever reason, your past self wasn't ready for this challenge. If you try again and persevere, you might be ready to complete it, or you might not.

It's not healthy to beat yourself up over the goals you didn't accomplish in the past. To persevere with your current goals, you need to shed any guilt from the past and focus on the project at hand. If you decide to put down your current goal, remember that you can always pick it back up again.

Wayne, one of our earlier examples, lost his house and all his belongings in a horrible earthquake/flood/fire combination. Instead of moving forward with his goals, Wayne decided to put them down for a while so he could focus on taking care of his basic necessities, such as housing and food. Wayne is not quitting his goals; he's setting them to one side so he can focus on getting his life back in order. He shouldn't feel guilt or shame for taking care of himself. The moment he has his basic necessities under control, Wayne can dive back into his goal setting.

Perseverance also includes being smart with your time and resources, so make sure to take care of yourself, and the goal setting will come with time. Reward yourself for the little milestones and keep pushing forward. You've got this!

Chapter Six:
Evaluating Your Progress

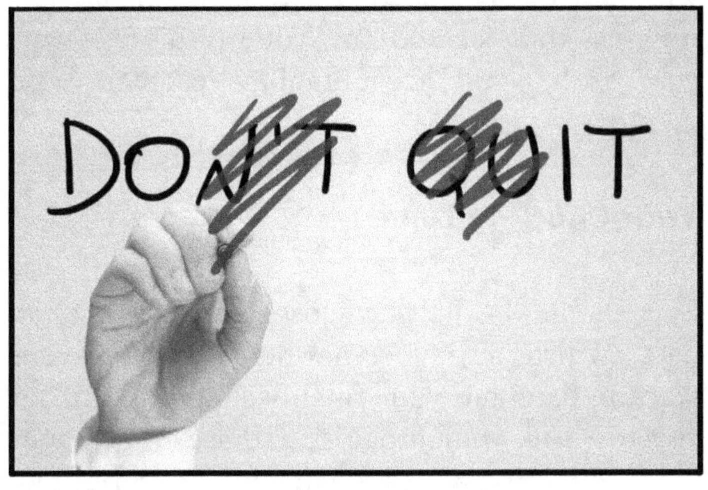

So you've come this far, your goals, accountability partners, and mentor in tow, and now you're hopefully beginning to see some progress. If you don't like planning stuff in advance, you've still been able to focus on the big picture and get stuff done. Also, if you don't mind scheduling your time in detail, you've been killing it with all those checklists under your belt. Everything has been going well, just like you planned. Right?

Regardless of whether you're feeling proud of yourself or shaking your head in embarrassment, you will have to face the fact that your deadline is approaching, and you want to reach the end of your journey. Let's take this time to look at your progress thus far and how you can discuss your goal with your accountability partners and mentor.

Your Check-in Date

You should be getting close to your check-in date, which a day somewhere between your starting date and your final deadline, meant for you to check your progress and see what issues you need to fix, what growth you've experienced, and most importantly, if you can finish your goal on time. If you're not even close to your start date yet, don't worry—you can still read this chapter and get an idea of what you should do when you reach the halfway mark.

When you reach the halfway point of your goal, it might be clearly halfway done, or it could be more difficult to discern your progress. As we covered in chapter one, your goals shouldn't be vague because when it's too hard to track your progress, you will be more likely to get discouraged and stop working on your goals. When your goal is something measurable, you can probably tell if you are halfway done just by looking at your checklist or listening to your heart. However, it's also a good idea to get the input of others and ask for their advice in case you missed something important.

This chapter is all about your check-in date. First, we will talk about how to check your own progress, and we will check in with some of our examples from earlier chapters and how we can track their progress. Then, we'll discuss how to check in with your mentor and accountability partners.

Finding the Halfway Mark

What is the easiest way to know if you are progressing at the right speed? What should you aim for when you reach the halfway mark, and what do you do if you're nowhere close to being on track?

Every goal has its own unique halfway point that is determined by you, your specific goal, and the amount of progress you want to get done before your deadline. Physical goals about your health require different methods for tracking progress than career goals or even emotional and spiritual goals. Your situation is unique to you and where you are at this point in your life. Because each situation is unique, we will go over some specific examples to demonstrate some of the strategies you can use to measure your goals.

Brenda is trying to start a cake decorating business, and her goal is to serve fifty customers in the next six months. After three months of practicing, advertising, and frosting birthday cakes for her neighbors, Brenda reaches her check-in date and looks at her progress. She doesn't have 25 customers yet, so she's not quite halfway to her goal of fifty customers, but she is making a lot of great progress. For instance, 18 of her 21 customers found out about her in the past month. So, Brenda could choose to feel discouraged and say she's behind schedule, or she could realize that her business growth is just beginning and she will find success if she sticks with her plan.

Marie wants to be a better mother to her children, and her main goal is to stop yelling at her kids when she gets angry. She's progressing just fine, and her family is impressed with the improvement, until the night before her check-in date when Marie finds two of her children coloring on a treasured family heirloom with sharpies. Marie loses it and starts screaming at the kids before sending them straight to their rooms. When the kids are in bed, Marie breaks down in tears, believing she failed her goals and her children. On one hand, Marie could feel discouraged and say she has to start over because she yelled at her kids; on the other hand, this was not a goal that she could measure with one success or failure at a time, but by an average. Since the average is Marie is yelling less, she is still making good progress and she shouldn't have to start over from the bottom.

Are We There Yet?

Goals that are more abstract or lengthy will be more forgiving if you're behind the halfway point by your check-in date. Your halfway point doesn't have to be perfect; however, if you have a measurable goal (such as weight loss or a calorie-specific diet), you will want to be as close to the halfway mark as possible. Let's say your goal is to lose ten pounds before summer, which you officially define as June 21st. By the halfway mark, you should lose between four and six pounds to be on track to meet your goals. It's not healthy to lose a lot of weight too quickly, so the halfway mark can act as a way to protect yourself from a last minute rush of losing weight too quickly and unhealthily to meet the deadline.

It's common to feel like you're a little behind at this point, and that's okay, so long as you have made progress since your first day. You can play catch up, or you can rearrange your approach, but it's hard to start from a blank slate. It's okay to be one-third of the way through or even one-quarter of the way, as long as you have something to work with.

After examining your starting point and the point where you'd like to end up, is your current situation somewhere in the middle? What would you define as the halfway point of your goal, and do you believe you're there yet? If not, how soon will you be there?

Once you determine the answers to these questions, it's time to delve a little deeper and examine how you feel about your progress. Write down your answers to these questions somewhere, be it a notepad, a whiteboard, a notebook, or on your computer, because the act of writing can change how you process information, making it easier to remember.

- On a scale of 1 to 10, with 10 being the finish line, how far would you say you've progressed in your goals?

- Are you checking items off your goal checklist (or your mental checklist if you don't have an explicitly written checklist)? How many subgoals and steps have you completed?

- How happy are you with your success so far? Are you taking the time to congratulate and reward yourself when you complete small steps? Rewarding yourself for a job well done is one of the best ways to beat procrastination and achieve your goals.

- Is there an aspect of your goal that you didn't expect or that you didn't know about ahead of time? How can you deal with this unexpected challenge in the future?

- Is your goal still the right one for you?

Nobody will grade your answers unless you decide to share these questions with your accountability partners, so be as honest as you can. By thinking about these questions now, you are pushing your brain to evaluate your current status, which will come in handy when it's time to tell your accountability partners about your progress.

How to Go Crazy in Less than 24 Hours: Playing Catch Up

When the holidays roll around, an emergency hits, or procrastination takes root in your life, it's way too easy for us to hit the snooze button on our dreams and focus on anything except our goals. I know this because I used to be a chronic procrastinator. We turn to anything that gives our brains a new problem to focus on, and since our brains are pretty lazy, we don't like to refocus ourselves. Instead, we continue hitting that proverbial snooze button while we put our dreams off for a day, a week, or even a month.

One day, your phone buzzes with a new notification from your Google calendar. In all caps, it says, "CHECK IN WITH ACCOUNTABILITY PARTNERS." You let out a loud, unhappy groan. Your world of other important things has been interrupted, and now you have a choice to make: should you turn off the notification and hit snooze on your dreams one more time, or should you accept the wake up call from your past self and start working on your goals again?

It's been three weeks since you did anything that you could consider as working on your goals, but on the inside, you feel guilty about letting your goals sit this long for no real reason. Therefore, you accept the challenge, and you decide to play catch up and get yourself back on track. Depending on your goal, this could be a recipe for success or a foretelling of disaster.

Playing catch up on your goals is not always the best idea. I highly recommend letting your accountability partners know that you're having a change of plans, then sitting down and reworking your goal to fit your schedule better. What part of your goal was difficult to persevere with? How can you make it better the second time through? You should adjust your deadline when needed to avoid cramming too much work into one day and potentially harming yourself. For example, you can submit thirty job applications in a week in an attempt to catch up with your goal, but you cannot and should not expect to lose thirty pounds in a week, and in doing so, you could cause a lot of damage.

If you aren't anywhere near being halfway through your goal at this point, talk it over with your accountability partners and get their advice on what you should do next. For most people, this means you'll need to adjust your deadline and fix your goal plan.

Meeting With Your Accountability Partners

Now that you have evaluated your current progress and how you feel about your success thus far, it's time for you to meet with your accountability partners and discuss your goals with them. Don't let yourself or anyone else put off this meeting—if they can't meet with you in person, see if you can set up a twenty minute phone call or even simply send them an email. This is your deadline to meet your halfway mark, and if you put it off until another day, it might not happen at all. It's important to do it now while it's fresh in your mind.

In the case of someone with multiple accountability partners, individual, one-on-one meetings are usually best unless all of the accountability partners are friends and work together well. Here's some ideas for how to meet up with an accountability partner:

- **Take them out to lunch**. By and large, people love food, especially if someone else is paying.

- **Grab coffee with them**, which could still be effective and much less expensive than lunch.

- **Meet them at a local bookstore or library**. This option is usually better for people who are more motivated in holding you accountable, as there's no free food involved. Either way, it's a great place to talk because bookstores and libraries are usually quiet.

- **Invite them on a hike with you**. Be sure to check the local weather forecast and pick a hike that's relatively easy, so both of you can focus on the conversation.

- **Host them in your home and offer them some homemade cookies**.

- **Is there something related to your goal that you could be doing**? Maybe you need to go to a park and do some walking, or you need to go pick up your new business cards. You could probably meet them right afterwards, and it will remind them that you're actively working on your goals.

- Depending on the ages of any children you may have, **ask if the kids want to have a playdate** while the adults talk about goals.

These were just some ideas to get you started, and this list is by no means exhaustive. Call or text your accountability partners and see what works for them. Again, if they are too busy on your official check-in date, ask them whether you could send them an email or give them a phone call.

Part of setting a check-in date for yourself is so that you can benefit from the added accountability. The check-in date says not only will you have accountability partners, but you will talk with them on that specific day and update them on your progress. So, as much as it is in your power, try to meet with your accountability partners on this day or at least send them an email update.

Once you set up a time and a place to meet, you need a plan for what you want to discuss. Of course, you won't be giving them a speech or conducting a high-stress interview, but it is a good idea to map out a few of your questions beforehand so you don't forget to ask anything important.

What Do I Talk About With My Accountability Partners?

So, what kind of things should you talk about with your accountability partners? Your discussion shouldn't be scripted or forced, however, it's a good idea to bring up certain topics that you need help on.

Brock is progressing well toward his goal of becoming a store manager. He has the training he needs and he's applied to multiple jobs, two of which have already contacted him and asked for an interview. Some questions Brock might have for his accountability partners include:

- *(To his friends) What do you think is the best job interview advice most people don't know about? What is something you learned about interviews the hard way? Do you know anything about how they hire people at x company?*

Notice that Brock probably knows how to do well in a job interview if he's worked other positions before. Don't be afraid to ask questions to which you might know the answer too because you might hear some great advice you didn't know about before. For example, let's say one of Brock's friends replies, "My uncle used to work at x company as a manager and he would never hire anyone who said y." Brock would have missed out on that if he didn't ask about job interviews.

- *(To his wife)* Which tie should I wear to the job interview?

In many cases, women are considered better at matching colors and outfits than men. Of course, this depends from person to person, but in this example, we'll assume that Brock's wife is much more color savvy than he is. Also, his wife may be more familiar with his closet than anyone else who could give Brock fashion advice.

- *(To his family and friends) What do you think my next step should be? What could I be doing better?*

Brock's friends are close enough to him that they will be able to give him constructive criticism. These will be the questions he wants answered the most, so he asks everyone.

As you think about what to ask your accountability partners, keep the questions light. Tell them about your current progress, including setbacks and struggles you've faced, then ask for their advice and what they would do in your place. Many people like to share their opinions, so you can't really go wrong asking detailed questions about their feedback.

Here are some more ideas for questions you could ask:

- *Do you think I'll meet my goal by this deadline? (you can tell them it's okay to say no). Why or why not? Do you think I could get it done sooner? Should I change my deadline?*

- *How can I be more productive in the second half of the project? What are some ways I could stop procrastinating so much?*

- *Could you text/call/email me every so often to check in on my progress?*

- *How should I celebrate when I reach my goal?*

Remember, this is your chance to ask for advice and ideas in a friendly manner. If your accountability partners will have some constructive criticism for you, so take note, as they probably don't say these things lightly. They know that you're counting on them to provide accountability, and if they notice something that you need to change, they will let you know. Thank them for their honesty and don't say anything to defend yourself; just take their advice and recognize that they're only saying these things to help you.

In the case that no one thought you needed to change anything, and you came away from the conversation with no additional ideas, feel free to move ahead as planned. However, if you did receive constructive criticism, take some time to adjust your plans and checklist and continue moving forward.

Meeting With Your Mentor

For more focused, specialized advice, now is the perfect time to consult with your mentor. This is your chance to ask the questions that your accountability partners didn't know the answers to, and the questions that left them scratching their heads.

Don't be afraid to ask your mentor hard questions to see what they say. They're human too, meaning they might not know the answer; however, their level of insight will probably be a bit higher than that of your accountability partners (after all, that was why you chose them as your mentor in the first place, right?).

The goal of this check-in meeting is to ask for your mentor's advice on how they would proceed, and whether you need to change any part of your tactic. Start by letting them know that you appreciate their time and you just wanted to check in with them regarding your goal, and you wanted to know if they had any other advice or concerns.

For example, while Brock asks more casual questions to his friends and family, he can ask his mentor (a former manager of *x* company) more detailed questions about the hiring process, a typical day working at *x* company, and the most challenging aspects about working for *x* company. He might not receive answers to all his questions due to company policy, but when talking with his mentor, Brock will have a higher chance of hearing information that he can use to guide his future steps.

Consider this check-in meeting like a second starting line—you've come halfway, now gather yourself and get ready for the final stretch. Your mentor and accountability partners will be there to guide and help you along the way, so listen closely to their advice and keep moving forward. In doing so, you will reach your final destination before you even know it.

The Halfway Mark Reward Station

Once you've made it this far, and your accountability partners all agree that you're about halfway to the finish line, it is now a good time to spend quality time with yourself and feel proud about your accomplishments. In fact, research has shown that if you reward yourself for working on your goals, you will be more likely to succeed. Therefore, go ahead and treat yourself at the halfway mark, maybe not with your final reward, but something almost as good. Here's a few ideas for you to try:

- **Sleep in on a Saturday morning**.

- **Buy and download a new game on your phone or tablet**.

- **Cook some of your favorite breakfast foods from scratch, no matter if it's breakfast time or not**. Pancakes, biscuits and gravy, and baked apples are almost tastier for dinner than for breakfast because your brain isn't expecting them.

- **Have a Netflix show marathon or a movie marathon**. The trick with this one is to make sure that you're watching movies or shows that you've already seen, so if you fall asleep on the couch while you're watching them, all the better! Grab yourself some popcorn and make a pillow fort for an extra cozy feel.

- **Take a hot shower or a bath**.

- **Put on your walking shoes and go outside**. See how far you can walk. It isn't a race, so you can stop as often as you want to. If you live in a city, you might be surprised by the places and shops you never noticed from inside your car. If you live in the country, you can enjoy the scenery and soak in the fresh air. When you're done, you can either walk home or get a ride back to your house from a loving spouse, friend, or family member.

- **Listen to a podcast**.

- **Re-read your favorite book, cover to cover**.

- **Visit a nearby animal shelter and pass out treats to the animals**. Often, shelters have treats that you can give to the animals, or you can bring your own. Be sure to double check with the staff members about their policy on treats.

- **Invite friends and family over for a game night**. Everyone can bring their favorite games and a snack to share.

- **Take a power nap**. Twenty minutes of napping is amazing for alertness. The best time to power nap is between 1 and 4 pm.

Once you reward yourself for making it this far, keep pushing ahead with your goals! You have an awesome reward waiting for you at the finish line.

When you do accomplish your goal, go ahead and read the next chapter, "Achieving Success," because that's what you will be doing: achieving success.

Chapter Seven: Achieving Success

Welcome to chapter seven, the chapter in which we talk about *parties!* By this point, you have completed or at least made a good deal of progress toward your goals. On the other hand, you might be reading ahead to get a sneak peek at what happens in the last chapter, or you might be casually looking through this book and you still haven't started working on your goals because you're trying to decide if it's worth it.

In an ideal world, you focused, you persisted, you persevered, and now, you're close to finishing your goals. It's common by this point to feel lots of emotions: excitement, accomplishment, relief, or complete energy drainage. The more work you poured into accomplishing this goal, the more likely you are to feel emotionally drained after meeting your deadline. But now, it's time to celebrate your success!

What If I Don't Succeed?

If you didn't meet your goal the first time through, go back to your plan and figure out what went wrong. When you restart an old goal, don't keep pushing ahead if the first try didn't go so well because you'll be setting yourself up for disappointment. Instead, it's time to reevaluate. Ask yourself the following questions:

- Did I plan too much or not enough? Did I pick the scheduling style that fits me best or did I choose the wrong one? Don't underestimate yourself. A lot of people believe they hate setting schedules, when in reality, they struggle with procrastination, and setting a planned routine will help them be more productive.

- Was this goal realistic? If not, can I change it or scale it back to make it more attainable?

- What kept me from achieving this goal? How can I get around this setback in the future?

I cannot emphasize this point enough—there is no such thing as a complete failure in the world of goal setting. You can choose to set aside a goal for a day, a week, or even five years, but you haven't failed. It's always okay to come back and try again later.

If you've come this far without completing your goal, it's never too late to keep improving yourself. The brain is built to view an unfinished goal as a failure. Most of the time, this thinking makes it extremely hard to work on old, unfinished goals because we already think of them as a waste of time. However, by attempting a goal more than once, you have a chance to improve your strategies with each fresh start. If one step took you three weeks longer than you expected, see if there's a way to avoid that step or make it easier to complete. If you gave up because you struggled with procrastination, remind yourself to stay productive and increase the number of times you reward yourself.

Never view unfinished goals as failures because that's not what they are. Unfinished goals are simply unfinished goals; it's your choice to decide whether you want to finish them in the future.

I've Accomplished My Goal, Now What?

Take a moment to close your eyes and think about how far you've come to get to this point. You met your goal, and now it's time to celebrate that accomplishment. Doesn't this moment feel amazing?

Remember this moment of triumph. By accessing this memory in the future, when you feel like giving up, you can remind yourself of why you're setting goals in the first place. You want to improve some aspect of your life, and you want to achieve something by setting this goal; therefore, it's important for you to complete it.

As we discussed in previous chapters, every goal needs a great reward by the end. When you complete a large project, your brain expects payment for its trouble, and there are many ways that you can set up a healthy, effective award without destroying your previous work. We covered some reward ideas at the end of chapter one, and then again in chapter six.

If you have successfully completed your goal, go ahead and treat yourself. Now is your time to celebrate! However, before you leave, go ahead and say the following sentences out loud. You can say them to your Google Home device, your cat, the nearest houseplant, or even another human being, but the act of talking out loud will give your brain powerful signals that can help you believe what you're saying. Read these statements proudly:

- I am smart enough to make decisions about myself and my situation.

- I am strong enough to pursue my goals and complete them.

- I am valuable and I can improve myself because I'm worth it.

These statements are good to review many times, but they're especially good to tell yourself right now when you have a chance to believe them 100%, since you just finished a big milestone. Give your brain some credit at the end of a difficult journey, and make sure to leave room in your morning routine to uplift yourself, not just today, but every day.

Once you have read those three statements out loud, go ahead and give yourself that reward.

Reward Rain Checks

If the weather or your financial situation gets in the way, don't skip your well-deserved reward; you don't want to give your brain any reason to avoid goal setting. The following are some last minute reward ideas.

Julie achieved her goal of getting hired to work with Disney, which is her dream company. She originally planned to take herself out to the movies as her reward, but an unexpected ice storm interrupted her plans. Instead of going to the movies, Julie can bundle up in her favorite blankets, light some candles, and give herself a manicure. She could also treat herself to a reading marathon, where she reads all her favorite scenes from her favorite books with a brief pause to mix up some egg-free cookie dough to snack on. Of course, once the roads are safe and the power comes back on, Julie can go to the movies and follow through on her promise to herself.

Leo sold his first novel to a publisher. His original plan was to go see a major league baseball game once the novel was sold, but before he could buy himself a ticket, his mother had an emergency and Leo spent all his money on a plane ticket to go take care of her. After arriving back home again, the baseball game had already happened, and Leo didn't get to go. Leo, however, still has several options. He could pick up a couple of odd jobs and save the money to buy a ticket to next week's game, or he could go for a bike ride through downtown or along the beach. He could also visit the mall, grab a soda from the food court, and spend the afternoon people watching. In doing so, might even find some inspiration for his next book.

What if your original reward wasn't exciting enough? You finished your goal, only to feel underwhelmed when you give yourself that reward you'd been waiting for. In this case, add another reward for yourself. If you completed a goal, you deserve to feel amazing about it afterward!

For example, Carl finally lost that forty pounds that his doctor has been bugging him about for years. He originally planned to celebrate by taking the day off, but after he finished his day off, it felt like something was still missing. Since his weight loss took him so long to accomplish, he felt like his original reward wasn't good enough. To compensate, he picks something a little bit bigger, like a date night with his wife at a fancy restaurant. He could also go shopping for new clothes to fully appreciate his weight loss progress.

However you choose to reward yourself, make it so enjoyable that you start thinking, "I want to do this for myself more often!" This is an excellent motivator that you might decide to use again in the future.

Using Dopamine (The Healthy Way)

When you set goals, you don't always have to indulge in large, expensive rewards for yourself. The brain's reward system is dopamine, which, if you manage properly, can change your entire outlook on life. When you mentally congratulate yourself for completing tasks, you give yourself a little shot of dopamine, which keeps your brain engaged and energized, similar to a shot of espresso.

By engaging in healthy pep-talks with yourself and rewarding yourself for each task you accomplish, you're training your brain to enjoy the process of goal setting. While the brain automatically releases dopamine when you have sex, consume sugar and caffeine, and play online games, it won't reward itself for hard work unless you train it to do so.

You should never abuse the use of your body's natural hormones, but when you train your mind to enjoy reaching goals, the process of goal setting will grow easier over time. Also, avoid using addictive substances like drugs, sugar, and caffeine to release dopamine. Doing so can dull your brain, and your brain will have to release larger and larger amounts of dopamine to get the same feelings, which is the basis of addiction.

Celebrating small achievements will increase your chances of success because you will reach a place where you love to set goals. Start with celebrating the small tasks, and eventually, you will find that you enjoy the bigger tasks too. After all, who doesn't love to treat themselves after a hard day's work?

Breaking the Good News to Your Accountability Partners

Since they are the people who have supported you through your goal setting endeavors, while also being the people who agreed to hold you accountable and check in on your progress (or at least endure your hourly updates), your accountability partners have a right to know when you have completed your goal. In fact, if you shared your deadline with them, you may have also prompted a few of them to ask, "Are you done with that goal of yours yet?"

Yes, you are done with your goal, and it's time to let them know.

There are several different ways to do this, and the decision is yours to make in the end. How you reveal the news depends on the type of goal, your level of comfort with these people, and whether they know each other. Here's a few ideas to get you started:

- **Call each of them on the phone and tell them the news**—This is great for if your goal is related to pregnancy, weight loss, a new job, or something so significant that the other person can immediately exclaim, "Wow, that's so exciting! Congratulations!"

- **If calling people on the phone is not your thing, try texting them**—When you switch to the written word, it becomes much less formal, so it could be a better fit for most goals.

- **Send out a group email and send each of your accountability partners a BCC** (blind carbon copy)—This option works well if your accountability partners don't know each other, but you still want to save time by telling them all at once.

- **If you decide to send them a small gift (such as a gift card) for their help, send it to them with a fun greeting card**—This is a great idea for if your accountability partners acted as your mentors and gave lots of thorough advice.

- **Meet with them and tell them the news in person**—You achieved your goal! This can be anything from a low-key conversation at work to inviting the squad over for a party, and it is the best way to let everyone know about your success. It also gives them a chance to give you some parting words of advice or guidance before they consider the case closed.

Again, a good deal of how you share the news depends on the nature of your goal. I'll share some examples of what you could say in different situations, but in many cases, you could simply blurt out the news and it won't make any difference. These are just some examples of how you might open the discussion in different settings:

- **Get straight to the point**—"I've officially gone two months without a cigarette."

- **Say it subtly**—"I had a meeting with the manager of company *x* today... I should say, my new manager."

- **The tried and true attention-grabbing method**—"Guess what?" And wait for them to guess.

You might consider involving your accountability partners in some part of your rewards. Again, who's to say you can't have more than one reward? Feel free to research some inexpensive activities in your area, whether that's a free museum or a food truck festival, and invite them to join you. They will appreciate the invitation.

Also, be sure to thank your mentor for all of their help and guidance. A thoughtful gesture would be to send them a handwritten note in the mail and perhaps a gift card to their favorite restaurant. This step isn't required, but it's a nice way to thank them for their time, and is also a way to tell them the exciting news about your success.

Don't Rest on Your Laurels

So, you finished your first goal. That's a huge milestone, and it's something most people won't even attempt, but you did, and you pushed through all the way to the end.

However, after you take some time to relax and reward yourself, you still have one more decision to make.

- You could put this book down and never set another goal in your life; or

- You could celebrate your success, go back to page one of this book, pick a new goal, and continue growing yourself physically, mentally, emotionally, and spiritually.

At the end of the day (and the end of the book), the choice is ultimately yours to make, but I encourage you to keep setting new goals. The more you are intentional about improving your life, the better chance you have at reaching success and finding happiness.

In the days of Ancient Greece, someone who won a race in the Olympics was awarded a **crown of laurels**. To them, this was the equivalent of a gold medal. Resting on your laurels meant that you relaxed too long, ruining your past achievements. You don't want to let your career, health, or relationships slide backwards and have to set the same goal four times.

The easiest way to stop resting on your laurels is to set yourself a new goal and continue moving forward. Every person on Earth has room for improvement, and you can never be too good at goal setting. Continue to strive for improvement, and over time, achieving your goals will become second nature to you.

Remember, no matter how old you are, what your financial situation is, or what your life goals are, if you set goals and achieve them, you will have all the tools you need to succeed.

Moving Forward

Over the course of this book, we have learned how to come up with goals and evaluate them to see which ones are worth pursuing. We discussed how to set deadlines, create a plan of action that fits our personal planning style, and how to approach people to be your mentor and accountability partners. We also covered how to overcome procrastination, persevere through the tough times, and how to evaluate your progress at the halfway point. Finally, in chapter seven, we discussed what happens after you achieve your goals.

I said *when*, not *if*. The key to success is positivity. Various scientific studies have proven that positivity is linked with higher levels of perseverance and productivity; therefore, if you stay positive when times get tough, you are better equipped to find alternate routes that most people would have missed altogether. You open your own eyes to see the best in every situation. With a positive outlook on life, you give yourself the key to success.

When you use a positive attitude to control your actions, you will take control of your own life. Not everything that happens to you is under your control, but your growth will be, and if you don't grow, you will miss out on all the richness that life has to offer. By pressing through the bad times, the difficult goals, and the past failures, your growth can truly begin.

Goal setting has so many positive effects on the other areas of your life, including:

- Increased motivation.

- More self-control and personal discipline.

- More satisfaction from everyday life.

- A better sense of purpose.

- The best chance of getting the future you want.

Like any other habit, goal setting might take a while to learn and adapt into your routine. To make goal setting an integral part of your routine, try using these proven methods to change your habits.

- **Keep doing it every day for thirty days**. Depending on the habit, it could take anywhere from twenty to sixty days for your brain to adapt to new habits and behaviors. You'll see better results if you choose a certain time each day to work on your goals.

- **Write down a brief description of what you want this habit to look like**. For some people, this might mean working on their goals for thirty minutes every evening. For others, they might be unable to commit to much more than five minutes during their lunch break. Figure out what works for you and write that down.

- **Start small and simple**. Don't try to change your entire routine in one fell swoop unless you have to. If you want to spend thirty minutes a day working on your goals, start by spending ten minutes per day and work your way up. If you want to wake up an hour earlier than you do now, wake up fifteen minutes earlier each day until you reach the time you're looking for. You don't want your body and mind to rebel against the new habit by forcing them into it too quickly.

The act of setting aside some time for your goals can be a goal by itself. Make sure to reward yourself after you spend thirty days setting this habit.

Your success in ultimately in your hands, which can be an exciting reality if you know how to wield it. You need to know how to set and achieve goals, so you don't live with regrets. You don't want your life to control you—you want to control your life. The way you do that is through goal setting, hard work, and defeating procrastination.

Where do you go from here? I'll leave that question up to you. I hope you found this book to be a source of wisdom and helpful information for all things related to goal setting, and I hope that you have completed your first goal by this point, or you're at least well on your way to achieving it.

Every day, I am constantly learning how to set goals that will change my life and the lives of others around me. I hope that you'll join me on this journey. Once you start setting and reaching new goals, each one will become easier and easier to plan and achieve. I truly and sincerely believe that if you can get to the point where goal setting is a part of your lifestyle, you will take yourself far in this life, and you will be able to do anything you set your heart on.

Book 2:
Productivity Plan

How To Rewire Your Brain, Build Better Habits, And Overcome Procrastination With 31 Life Hacks

Introduction

If you suffer from procrastination, you are not alone. Some estimate that one in five is a procrastinator, and that number has been increasing. A study done in 1978 showed 5% of the student population admitted to being procrastinators. Enter the era of being fashionably late, and by 2007, that number jumped to 26%. Holy moly, that's a significant increase!

Is it just a first world problem? Primarily, yes. In our fast-paced society where efficiency and productivity are prized commodities, individuals implode and ruin their careers because they put off important deadlines or just fail to jumpstart themselves in a timely way. In the cutthroat world of competition, these people don't lose out because others are better, smarter or more worthy...they lose out because of self-demolition. Their behaviors are self-destructive.

The phenomenon is so common they have earned their own monikers. Known as procs or members of the big P society, they earn negative attention and the process reinforces the underlying thought processes causing their procrastination, and the cycle just keeps repeating itself. What is needed is a whole new mindset.

You picked up this book because you thought, Maybe, just maybe, there's an explanation or cure for me. If that's the case, you are right. You are 100% right. The destructive cycle of procrastination can be broken, and you can set your life in order. I am a world class recovering procrastinator, and living proof that change is just one month away. Thirty-one days to a better you. Does it sound too good to be true?

It's not. Your brain has been wired for defeat and we're about to rewire it for success. We're going to form new habits. Reprogram old thought patterns. Build confidence. You are thirty-one days from having your boss, your companion, your friends noticing a change in you, but do you know what? You'll be the first to see the change, and it will feel soooo good. Don't be surprised if it is reflected in the way you dress or the way you carry yourself. The confidence gained from taking control of your mind is no little thing. You are worth investing in, and that's exactly what you'll be doing.

From the first day's reading and writing assignment through the last of the thirty-one days of hacks, you'll be investing your time and your mind into a project we'll call the new and improved you. Let's imagine what that looks like. Bear with me...imagine what you'd wear to a business meeting or interview or appointment where you knew you'd be knocking the socks off everyone you'd meet along the way or find sitting across from you at the table. Imagine your expression. Is it one of cocky self-promotion (often associated with those who seriously doubt themselves) or one of self-assurance? This. This is the new you we're aiming to produce.

Let's make a pact. I won't give up on you, if you won't give up on yourself. Can you agree to that? Thirty-one days to a better you? I know. You're a procrastinator, and you have trouble digging in...but something made you pick up this book, and I've got to believe that you are ready for a change. If that's true, get out your calendar. Mark off thirty-one days. Decide on a time of day for doing the insanely easy work of rewiring your brain. Decide on a reward.

Let's say you're going to dig in at 10:00 pm every night. That's your quiet time for personal reflection. Get out your book and your paper and pen. Do your chapter. Put a star in the calendar. Eat that bowl of ice cream or play that video game. Don't forget to reward yourself. You deserve it! Perhaps your best time is 7:00 am, and then you must dash to work. No problem. You can mark off your calendar in the evening and reward yourself during happy hour. Do you see the key point I'm getting at here?

Change never occurs in a vacuum. You must rewire the brain and that requires a welcome environment and lots of happy rewards. This book is not a drudgery. It's a happy place where you can revisit challenges and consistently improve, and each experience is associated with a reward you'll enjoy. Who wouldn't want to jump in and get started?

Let me assure you one thing. It's a promise from me to you. If you will do this, rewire your brain each day and reward yourself faithfully, you will become the you you've wanted to be for a very long time. Relationships will improve. Work will improve. Grades will improve. Most of all and the best part: you'll enjoy more satisfaction in life. Isn't that worth the change?

As great as accolades are, as much as we all enjoy promotions or raises, as much as being on the Dean's list is quite an honor, nothing beats the satisfaction of you knowing you are the person you have always wanted to be. That quiet confidence is all the reward you'll need. The other? It's icing on the cake, and who doesn't love icing? I'm excited to see the new you. Are you ready? Let's do it!

Part One:

How Procrastination Gets Wired Into Your System

Everyone procrastinates - or do they? While it is true that we've all been guilty of letting things slide once in a while, for most of us, it's simply that: an anomaly, not the norm. If you've picked up this book, you probably count yourself in another class of people: the class who procrastinates daily, for whom procrastination is an issue either at work, at school or in relationships or all three.

Chapter One:
Am I A Procrastinator?

Why do you suppose you put things off? Why do you suppose you have been unsuccessful in changing this habit? The #1 reason you can't kick the habit is because you don't label it for what it is. In this book, we will identify the many ways procrastination creeps in, what we call it, how it looks and what to do about it.

Recognizing that you procrastinate is the most important step in overcoming the stumbling block. You don't need a psychiatrist: this is one area where you can self-diagnose and save big bucks. You can self-treat to ultimate success.

Taking a tongue-in-cheek approach directly from Jeff Foxworthy, let's see how your brain is wired now:

- *You might be a procrastinator if* you fill your day with unimportant tasks on your checklist.

- *You might be a procrastinator if* you transfer the same important task to your to-do list six days in a row.

- *You might be a procrastinator if* you read your emails over several times without acting on any of them.

- *You might be a procrastinator if* you start a task and then end up making coffee. Caffeine is good, right?

- *You might be a procrastinator if* you fill your day with tasks you're doing for others, rather than getting your own work done.

- *You might be a procrastinator if* you're waiting to be in the mood to get the job done.

- *You might be a procrastinator if* you can't start until the time is juuuusssst right.

If you are a procrastinator, don't feel badly. You're in good company. Ten famous procrastinators may leave you feeling a little better about it all: The Dalai Lama, Bill Clinton, Franz Kafka, Saint Augustine, Frank Lloyd Wright, Leonardo da Vinci, Truman Capote and Margaret Atwood are all self-described procrastinators. Don't let that fool you into becoming complacent with your situation. Each of these people rose above that tendency to achieve excellence, and you can, too.

Roughly 20% of all adults and a whopping 46% of surveyed college students claim it has a negative impact on their happiness. The Procrastination Research Group at Carleton

University in Canada conducted an online survey, asking, "To what extent is procrastination having a negative impact on your happiness?" They found that one in two (46%) reported "quite a bit," and one in five (18%) reported it as having an "extreme negative effect." That means for them, it's transcended from a slip into a way of life, often with unhappy consequences. If you find yourself in this same boat, realize you don't have to stay there.

It's time to make a change, to become the person you want to be, to rewire your brain for success and happiness. Our 31 hacks to rewire your brain are meant to transform your thought processes and your actions into a new frame of reference.

Chapter Two:
What Does Your Faulty Wiring Look Like?

There are six types of procrastinators based on six different personality styles. As you read through these descriptions, you will identify with one or more of them. That signals exactly where your wires got crossed and, with that knowledge, we are going to untangle them and rewire your brain for your ultimate success.

Type One: The **perfectionist** doesn't want to start any task unless he/she can meet an exaggerated standard of quality. Some believe that perfectionism is the root cause of procrastination, but no, it's not. It's a myth, because research actually proves that perfectionists are less likely to be procrastinators. In reality, almost anyone can feel paralyzed when faced with postponed work, knowing they should start while being immobilized with anxiety. This is the *result,* not the *cause* of procrastination.

If you identify with the anxiety of not being able to start for fear it won't be good enough, this is good news. It means you can rewire your brain for success.

Don't get bogged down in details worrying about "the little things" like the type of font for your memos or where the calculator is for balancing your checkbook. One helpful strategy to worry less about details is conducting a reality check. Does it really matter? What is the worst possible outcome? Will this be important tomorrow? Next week? Next year?

Learn how to compromise with your inner self. How long do you think this task should reasonably take for completion? Could you agree to shave off one hour? Could you write a proposal now, and return to the subject to perfect it tomorrow? These little "deals" give you some insight toward lowering your own expectations.

What would it look like if you were less than perfect? Force yourself to make some conscious faux pas:

- Leave late for an appointment
- Leave a corner messy
- Admit to a weakness you would normally mask
- Wear a scarf that doesn't go with your suit
- Once a day, refuse to indulge in excessive behaviors, like constantly checking for errors

- Be late for an appointment once a day and make no explanations
- Buy a gift without researching the best deal

You can quiet the inner critic screaming at you by remembering that this isn't the demolition of your standards of excellence. It is reining them in so they don't control you. If this is hard, it's okay to ask for help. A friend or co-worker can help you talk through the areas where you may have focused too much importance and help you choose a non-critical area for practice. Last but not least, set a reasonable schedule.

By forcing yourself to moderate your own inner standards, you are wiring your brain for change. Each day try to increase the areas you choose to experiment in and let your inner critic learn to deal with it. Your anxiety will lessen over time and you will be able to self-monitor the paralysis that has made you a procrastinator. Look for more in-depth consideration in Part II at daily hack #1 and #3.

Type Two: The **dreamer** has all kinds of great ideas but considers carrying out the nitty-gritty details as such a downer. If you are this kind of procrastinator, you like the big picture and think in sweeping brush strokes. You are a visionary and, like most visionaries, happiest when others make your vision come to life.

In the real world of assignments and bosses and jobs to do, you have allowed your brain to get its wires crossed. Begin by striking certain words from your vocabulary. *Someday* and *I wish* need to go away. Instead, keep a planner handy and when you have an idea for a project, you may not know where to start. The dream remains a dream, and you reinforce your procrastinating habits.

Here are some ideas to start:

- Write down the steps to make your dream a reality, and don't worry about the order of importance.
- Prioritize these steps into a reasonable order for accomplishment.
- Put the steps into your schedule. Make self-realization a priority. Time block spaces to get specific goals accomplished.
- Chunk your dream into achievable bites and build on them. By building two priorities into a small pyramid, you will see progress a whole lot faster.

Use your ability to dream big to your advantage and don't let it paralyze you into inaction. Look in Part II for daily hack #13, #21 and #22 to practice your resolve.

Type Three: The **worrier** spends an inordinate amount of time on "what if" and gets caught in a self-perpetuating cycle of overthinking the situation. You may complicate the project with so many options that you don't know where to start. Your anxiety mounts as you try to think through every possible complication, leaving you mired at the starting gun while others are racing to the finish line. All of these behaviors demonstrate your propensity to worry, and hence procrastinate starting the project.

A lifetime of worrying will not disappear overnight, but you *can* rein in your tendencies and actually make this mindset work for you. It begins with a notepad, a pen and a cup of coffee. Let all those worries loose and jot them down. That's right. Get them out of your system. Once captured in black and white, it's easier to bypass the least important. Tackle one. Only one thing. Decide on one thing you can do to accomplish the assignment while satisfying this one projected outcome.

Make your worrying work for you as a form of quality control rather than letting it dominate you into a state of paralysis. Look at Part II life hack #1 and #6 for additional focus on this topic.

Type Four: The **crisis-maker** is an adrenaline junkie who thrives on the high of waiting until it's a last ditch effort salvation from disaster before tackling the project. You know this has spilled over into other parts of your life if you drive too fast, like extreme sports, shop late on Christmas Eve or prefer to debate on topics when they arise. Your procrastination is self-created as a way to producer another rush. It affects both your personal and professional lives and often results in destructive substance abuse.

It is also hard to combat because you justify your procrastination with a defense like, "I work better under pressure." What that really means is you don't like to work at all unless you are under pressure. All too often the result isn't your best work because you've squandered resources by waiting until the last possible moment. The work gets completed, yes, but you lacked time for review, editing the outcome and rumination over essential components. If you think you work better under pressure, imagine the outcome of a more deliberate presentation.

You won't cure your reliance on the adrenaline rush without deliberate effort but you can eliminate it as being the cause of your procrastination. Fixing this one small part of your life can reap big benefits professionally and may make it easier to transfer success into your personal life, as well. Look at Part II life hack #5, #11 and #16 to work on this trait.

Type Five: The **rebel** is often passive-aggressive and won't break the rules in open conflict but, by dragging their feet, manages to control the situation and defy expectations. Realize that no one is born passive-aggressive. It is a learned trait and affects your personal relationships even more profoundly than in a business setting.

You need to be ruthlessly honest with yourself to self-diagnose this tendency. It is often buried under layers of justification and while your boss, your companion, your friends, your family and your coworkers can spot it from a mile off, you may be blissfully unaware. Your reason for why you haven't started the project sounds righteous and you can rest secure in your position. If you analyze backwards, though, you will eventually admit to maybe feeling overlooked, maybe feeling humiliated by feedback or a number of other responses to negative interactions. You delay starting or finishing a project because in some way it affects those you secretly want to punish.

This is extremely difficult for the passive aggressive procrastinator to admit because in other social interactions it goes unnoticed. Kindness, talent and team spirit may be hallmark qualities 99% of the time, but not necessarily when it comes to starting or completing a project. Pay attention to Part II life hacks #7, #8, #11 and #19 to work on this quality.

Type Six: The **over-doer** does everything except his own assigned tasks, and leaves no time for his own work. The guilt of procrastination is mollified by all the good he's done for others but the boss won't be convinced and neither will his spouse.

You may harbor feelings of insecurity and feel

like you have to do more to merit respect and earn your way. An over-doer hates to ask for help. An over-doer is no stranger to hard work, because regularly spreading himself too thin increases his workload, which he is proud he can handle. This trait spills over into his personal life, robbing him of down time or time with a friend or companion. If you are an over-doer, you have trouble relaxing without justifying your down time. Does this sound like you?

The root of your action may be low self-esteem, and count on the work done to earn respect. This carries over into all parts of your life. You may not feel you deserve the home you live in, you may not feel a partner values you and feel jealousy, you are probably letting everyone and everything else control your priorities.

Take out a handy pad of paper and grab a pen and a cup of coffee. Write down your own goals, your own priorities. Realize no one gets to "have it all," and make the hard choices. Once you know what you really want in life, in business, in relationships, you can figure out the actionable items to achieve them. This holds true for projects as well as decisions on how to spend your bonus or tax return. Block time to satisfy your tasks. Learn to say no to requests that interfere with what makes *you* happy or what your boss or professor needs done.

Rewire your mindset daily by reaffirming certain truths:

- Life is a journey filled with adventure. Don't let it become a daily grind.
- You can't have it all but you can have what matters most.
- Don't look to others for extrinsic approval. Learn took at your daily actions and find completeness within yourself.
- Be sure to schedule leisure time because you

know you need to recharge your batteries.

Take heart by the fact that this type of procrastination is easy to remedy. What you need is an adjustment in priorities, not a kick in the rear. Look at life hack numbers thirteen, sixteen, twenty and twenty-four in Part II for exercises to help you solidify your change in mindset.

Recognizing your behavior, learning to be honest and how to self-evaluate, is the first step in rewiring your brain for success.

Chapter Three:
How Your Brain Got Its Wires Crossed

No one is a born procrastinator. That means that somewhere along the line your wires got crossed and we want to work together to rewire your brain to optimal function. To accomplish that goal, it is important to understand a little about how your brain works and how you became a procrastinator. It is worth taking a look at your owner's manual, rather than jumping in half-cocked and expending a lot of energy with few visible results.

Don't worry: This is something you can do all on your own. You don't need a therapist or group sessions. As a matter of fact, there is little evidence that therapy will help you because most of the professional literature a therapist utilizes is from very particular studies and focused on very specific situations making broad conclusions less clinically effective. A therapist prescribing treatment involves experimenting with common sense remedies you can institute and evaluate yourself.

The one function of a therapist you may want to implement is finding an accountability partner. Ask a friend or mentor to hold your feet to the fire as you work through this rewiring of your brain and you'll appreciate the savings in the process. This partner's role is not professional nor time-consuming. It's a matter of conversation. "How did you do on today's life hack?" "What was the most beneficial thing you did today?"

The value in going it alone is the inner strength you'll develop by not relying on a "professional." Learning to rewire your own brain in overcoming procrastination can be transferred to other life situations. You may apply many of these same principles to other situations with equal success, earning you handyman status extraordinaire.

You've probably gleaned from the last chapter how much I rely on writing things down. To proceed, I recommend a journal and a planner. Take notes on what resonates with you. Write down supporting quotes you like. Keep a record of your progress. Tackle your wiring project with all the detail and vigor as any other home improvement project, and you will not be disappointed with the results.

Ready to begin? Let's take a look at the handyman's review of the literature concerning wiring of the brain. The most basic definition of procrastination as defined by a number of psychologists always includes conflicted feelings between immediate gratification and the negative feelings associated with failure or delay. Translated, there always exists a tension between what you want most and what you want least. That's not so hard to understand.

You want recognition for a job well done but you don't want to do it wrong or do it now or do it poorly. If you want it done more than your fear of making a mistake, you begin immediately. If your fear of doing a poor job outweighs the gratification of getting it done, you procrastinate. This is not rocket science but if you listened to professionals, you might think it was!

The Premack Principle evolved from studying cerebus monkeys. Monkeys, really? It proved that they, like humans, would perform a small task to get a desired reward. It resulted in a fancy principle for something your grandma knew years ago. "Eat your veggies and you get dessert." See what I mean? This really isn't rocket science.

We will cover specific ways to decrease avoidance and increase gratification under daily life hacks in Part II. Realize right here is that your brain processes a million such conflicts each day without flaw. It short-circuits, though, when it comes to certain tasks or assignments and you need to rewire it for success when this happens.

Your brain functions fine 90% of the time; what derails it in these kinds of situations? Where did the wires get crossed? Your dysfunctional behavior when faced with a particular assignment is a result of self-regulatory failure. Sounds pretty fancy, so let's put it into everyday language. We control our own behavior to co-exist in society, living cooperatively and achieving our goals every single day. Self-regulation means you are able to choose from various alternatives, manage negative thoughts, control unruly impulses and the result is that everyone thinks you're normal.

There are two areas we want to look at in more depth. Managing negative thoughts is where a wire short circuits and loops destructively, paralyzing us into procrastination. What are these negative thoughts? Fear of failure, fear of asking for help, perfectionism, self-doubt, worry. These are giants we'll be slaying in Part II. Naming them, recognizing them is powerful. It is the first step in being able to look at each squarely in the eye and to stop the looping mechanism.

There is power in a name, a truth as old as time. Naming things lies at the basis of all creation stories, man trying to make sense of the universe. An ancient Chinese proverb says, "The beginning of wisdom is to call things by their right names." Isn't that true? If you can't identify the problem, you can't fix it. Perhaps English philosopher Francis Bacon said it best: "Knowledge is power." By recognizing and naming the undercurrent, you have already begun dismantling faulty wiring and are preparing to hardwire your brain for success.

Forms of decisional procrastination fall into this category. Over thinking, worrying over the outcome and fear of failure all trace their genesis to negative thoughts. Left unchecked, negativity spirals into other parts of your life.

Controlling unruly impulses is the other component of self-regulation required to rewire your brain. These impulses parade in front of us as distractions or more desirable opportunities. We marginalize the behavior with a tongue-in-cheek label of being a squirrel. These distractions pose a much more sinister role in your destructive behavior. Those impulses - to eat some chocolate, have another drink, go out with the gang and do your task later - result in procrastination. It sounds harmless when you're talking about a homework assignment worth ten points as opposed to a million dollar project your company is riding on but the result is the same.

By opting for immediate gratification over the task at hand, you are cementing habits that ultimately affect your success, a promotion, the happiness of your marriage, sometimes your health. The digital age feeds the whole pattern of instant gratification, making it a hard set of complicated wiring to fix within your brain. Not impossible. Realize how much you are feeding that impulse each and every day. It is being strengthened faster than you are dismantling it, unless you recognize and take some actionable steps to remedy the situation. You'll find a number of daily life hacks in Part II address this because it can grow out of proportion if left unchecked. This tendency to give in to instant gratification is the basis of behavioral procrastination. The life hacks to combat it include handling distractions, strategies to increase productivity, and developing new habits.

Our rewiring of your brain begins with conscious thought and is followed through with deliberate, repetitive action. It involves decision. It involves action. Looping these two components into a process you can replicate is the process of rewiring your brain for success. And that, friends, is how we cure our own proclivities toward procrastination.

Have you purchased that journal yet?

Are you ready to tackle this thing we call life and rewire your brain? As we proceed down this path together, you are *highly* encouraged to get a composition book and begin to journal. Use it to write down your goals, favorite quotes, ideas and new goals. Why journal? It is crucial to the process. I believe it is so important that I am going to bring it up again and in more depth.

As an inveterate journal-loving junkie, let me share some thoughts with you. I began journaling in high school and fell in love with capturing words on paper. At that time, I used a loose-leaf notebook with lined notebook paper. My next step into the wonderful world of journaling took a creative turn. Instead of notebook paper, I found decorative paper from an office supply store, punched holes in it and put it into a binder. Each day, I chose the paper that fit my mood, put a date at the top of the page and journal. At the end of each year I removed the pages, bound them together and started all over again.

Here's the key point: by journaling, I was able to go back and track my thoughts. Errant thoughts whirling around like tumbleweeds in my brain got tacked into place with words on the page. I could trace my progress through this life and grant it purpose. I am not alone.

Scientists recognize the benefits of putting words to the page. A group of researchers in 2013 discovered that 76% of adults who spend as little as twenty minutes a day journaling their thoughts, reacting to their feelings, heal faster than 58% percent of those who don't. They were looking at people being biopsied for medical diagnoses and saw ramifications for physical healing, an unexpected byproduct of journaling. If it does this for your body, think what it can do for your brain!

It leads to the conclusion that people who journal are healthier than their counterparts who don't journal, both physically and mentally. Journal keepers reap benefits that include improved mood and stress levels with less depression. They are less likely to get sick in the first place and tend to more successfully fight off disease, including conditions like asthma, AIDS and cancer.

To be effective, don't invest a huge time commitment to the process. Fifteen to twenty minutes a day over four months establishes the habit that produces measurable results. That's exactly the time bite we encourage you to invest each day as you work your way through this book, rewiring your brain one day at a time, in short bursts, consistently and persistently.

You may experience some upheaval throughout this process. Write it down. James W.

Pennebaker, a leading social psychologist at the University of Texas in Austin, says, "Emotional upheavals touch every part of our lives. You don't just lose a job, you don't just get divorced. These things affect all aspects of who we are -- our financial situation, our relationships with others, our views of ourselves...Writing helps us focus and organize the experience."

Here are twelve good reasons to begin journaling today. In this chapter. On this page.

1. It will be a means of capturing brilliance. Flashes of inspiration come and disappear like the scent of pizza when you're walking by a pizzeria. Don't lose them. After all, you may have to prove you're a genius to a friend or companion. What better way than documenting that brilliant idea?
2. Your journal is where you think big thoughts and dream big dreams. Everyone needs a

place to catalog errant dreams like being greeted at the White House or winning an award. It may be the only place you enjoy the experience and that's okay. Write it down.

3. Your journal is a place to wash the muddy windows of your mind. When you need clarity, write down the looping in your brain. It will help you see a path, find a solution, make a change.

4. A journal will help you change faster. It will become your user manual as you begin the rewiring process. Write down questions and you will find answers.

5. Keep track of your progress. Your insights on day 31 of life hacks will be more insightful than day 2. You earn that pat on the back by being able to document your rewiring.

6. Celebrate your progress. Your journal is a place to rejoice as you reap the benefits of rewiring your brain. Write down some praise you receive from your boss or the grade on a

project. Those quotes are the exclamation points of life. Don't lose them!

7. Your journal is your place to plan. Mentally strategize where you are going and how you plan to get there. Work through the process and you will see results.

8. In your journal you will be creating a routine of success. In your fifteen or twenty minutes each day, you will ponder, write, visualize and set goals. Do this for thirty-one days and create a pattern of success.

9. This is how you take control of your life. Instead of always being on the receiving end of life, become the person who makes your life happen. Deliberately. Successfully. Make the transformation from victim to victor as you rewire your brain.

10. What better reason to journal than to fatten your wallet? Ever heard the story about Jim Carrey writing himself a $10 million check before he achieved success in Hollywood? He

visualized where he wanted to be and then gave himself permission to strive for it. That's what a journal can do for you, whether your dream is owning your own home or driving a Lexus. Write it down in your journal and let the universe come to you.

11. Your journal is your therapist's couch, and believe me, it's a great savings over professional help. It's a place for complete honesty. A place to bare-knuckle brawl with your mind and whip it into shape. Your journal is your toolbox where the magic happens.

12. Last but not least, your journal is your means to establishing an attitude of gratitude. Write down things you appreciate and you'll begin to enjoy life as never before.

Before we go any further, get that journal!

Chapter Four:

How Procrastination Short Circuits Your Brain

Procrastination is affecting your brain and you see the results in your life. You may get passed over for a promotion you know you deserve - but your boss didn't know it. You may have gotten a B in a course when you know you deserve an A - but your professor didn't see it. As long as procrastination rules your life, you will continue to experience these disappointments.

Your brain's incessant looping leads to stress, depression, troubled relationships, a poor mindset, a lack-luster career and a poor reputation. That sounds serious, doesn't it? I'm as serious as a heart attack when I tell you that procrastination ruins lives.

Let's look at a case study or two. Linda became a procrastinator in her early adult years, and never addressed it. It became a looping pattern of passive aggressive behavior. She had trouble holding a job. Her husband and children learned to compensate by telling her to be somewhere at 5:00, when it actually began at 6:30. Eventually her husband left her, abandoning his ties to their extended circle of friends. One of her daughters disowned her. The other daughter set limits. And Linda still laments her life without any willingness to change. She suffered a widow maker heart attack and survived it, but nothing about her changed. She now faces an untimely move to a small apartment so her children don't have to mess with her. How sad. How sad, because at any point Linda could have opted to rewire her brain and change. But she didn't.

This happens to men, too. Dave is a dreamer. He often wistfully laments he should have been a musician but life didn't grant him that wish. Sigh. He controls others around him by controlling the pace of life. His boss let him go after thirty years of lack-luster performance. His children hate to work with him, because he wastes their time. He is living out his retirement years working at a poor paying job he hates because he lacked the wherewithal to change. A simple rewiring of his brain could have written a different ending.

Do you see bits and pieces of yourself, your own life story? If you feel under-valued, unappreciated, depressed over how your life is turning out, take note. These are the warning lights flickering on your console. It's time to rewire your brain. Do it before it defines your life and creates an unhappy ending. What are the effects of procrastination on the brain? Stress, depression, troubled relationships, a poor mindset, a lack luster career and a poor reputation. Let's explore these topics.

Stress

Stress is more than a sense of anxiety. We all feel anxious over looming deadlines, when we're pulled over by a cop, when we face a difficult situation. Here's a simple clue to determine if what you are experiencing is stress or anxiety: anxiety is situational. Stress remains when the situation is over. And the results of stress get imprinted in your body.

When your anxious moments turn to stress, your body tries to save you. It releases extra adrenaline to help you fight off whatever threatens you. Your adrenals secrete cortisol, the stress hormone, to improve cognitive function, fortify your immune system, lower your sensitivity to pain, increase glucose metabolism for spurts of energy and balance everything throughout the body. Those are good things, right? Well, those are good things if you are facing down a grizzly. Those are bad things when you are inviting them to stay and take up residence as the new norms in your life.

When chronic stress becomes the norm, a series of unfortunate results occur. Your tired body loses the ability to fight illness. Your worn out pancreas stops regulating insulin release and you become intolerant of glucose altogether, creating hypoglycemia and eventually, diabetes. Your tired body loses bone density. Your inflammatory system goes on red alert. Your blood pressure skyrockets and a host of diseases lead to more doctor visits as you fund his next year's vacation. Is this how you want to live?

The longer you live with chronic stress, the more you increase your susceptibility to addictive coping measures. Insomnia robs you of sleep. Your gut becomes unhealthy due to binge eating followed by not eating at all. You withdraw from friendships. Your immune system goes haywire and autoimmune diseases like fibromyalgia, arthritis and IBS become your new best friends. All this from procrastination?

Yes, I am afraid it is true. Psychologists call procrastination the most common form of self-sabotage and link it directly with stress. Think about it. You procrastinate a deadline to pick up some form of immediate gratification. You go to the movies, you visit with your friends, you take a weekend trip. Do you enjoy it? Always lurking at the back of your mind is the nagging remembrance that the deadline still exists. You *will* pay the piper. Your anxiety increases. Boom. Stress. Compound that scenario with a lifetime of procrastination and it's not hard to see why procrastination might be the root of *all* your stress.

Therapists love to treat your stress, but we want to eliminate the stress. We want to root it out and eliminate the problem. Here, you won't find any methods for lowering your stress level. No meditation. No motivational speeches about practicing peace. Going forward, we are going to decrease your stress level through daily life hacks: rewiring your brain at the source of the problem.

Depression

Depression is more than sadness. You get that, right? Sadness is situational. You feel sad because a friend moved away. You feel sad because a loved one died. You feel sad when you get laid off from a job you loved. Depression is a collection of sad feelings rolled into a syndrome with physical and psychological components. It lingers long after the sadness of the situation passes, and makes you wonder: *What's wrong with me?* Procrastination is a cause of depression.

Two problems people often profess are depression and procrastination, never connecting the dots. One is directly related to the other. Not getting things done, not meeting goals results in the feeling you aren't going anywhere and the negativity leads to depression, which fuels your procrastination. Somewhere you have to jump off that merry-go-round and address the problem at its source.

How do you know if you suffer from depression? Should you seek professional help? If your sad feelings and the following symptoms are pervasive and last longer than two weeks, you may want to consult your doctor. We will be removing depression at its genesis, but in no way would we dismiss your need for present help.

Signs you need help include:

- A depressed mood transcending much of the day characterized by sadness, feeling empty or hopeless, tears.
- Change of interest in activities you once enjoyed.
- Loss of weight when you're not dieting, or gaining weight as food becomes your source of comfort.
- Changes in sleep patterns.
- Fatigue, restlessness, a loss of energy.
- Feelings of guilt or worthlessness.
- Trouble concentrating.
- Thoughts of death or suicide.

To illustrate the difference, I'll share a personal example. When our son died, I experienced all of the above with the exception of suicide. It was directly related to the loss and lasted more than a year. I did not solicit help because it did not transcend into other parts of my life. I was not sad about my companion. I was not sad because of my friends. Being able to pin its genesis and gradual withdrawal from my life illustrated I was not clinically depressed.

There are many different types of depression: dysthymia (chronically low affect), postpartum depression, bipolar depression, seasonal depression, psychotic depression and treatment-resistant depression. These broad categories each manifest specific behaviors and each is treated differently. If you suspect any of these, you need to seek professional help.

Clinical depression involves the breakdown or loss of healthy neurotransmitters within the brain. It does require therapy and medical/professional intervention. Contrast that with the depression resulting from the consequences of your procrastination and you will see a pattern emerging. The negativity of your situation and lack of self-regulation is your problem, not an organic problem in your brain.. Let's rewire your impulses and remove the source of your problem through our daily life hacks.

Relationship Issues

Procrastination affects your relationships, and not in a good way. At the Latin root of the word, *pro* "in favor of" meets *crastinus* "of or belonging to tomorrow," signifying the loss of relationship many procrastinators miss. It's the gap between wanting love and postponing any behavior that might cultivate love. Many procrastinators self-sabotage their own relationships. The scenario is worse when procrastinators develop relationships with non-procrastinators.

Your roommate, your companion, your best friend often knows you better than you know yourself and, for better or worse, has to live with the consequences of your procrastination. Obviously, conflict ensues. Healthy relationships are built on mutual respect, teamwork and communication. When your behavior communicates a lack of respect and postpones mutually beneficial actions, your relationships understandably bear the brunt of your dysfunction.

Here are **four ways** your procrastination is impacting your relationships:

1. When you procrastinate, your friend or partner will feel resentment, lose trust in your commitment. A downward spiral develops. You feel badly. Your self-esteem suffers. Your stress level rises. This is a no-bueno for a healthy relationship.

2. When you procrastinate, your friend or partner loses trust in your willingness to follow through on commitments. Eventually, the trust level tips the relationship into crisis mode and it ends.

3. Procrastination results in wasted days and missed opportunities. Your friend or partner initially compensates by doing more. The result? You lose more self-esteem. Your relationship takes a nose-dive. Conversely, relationships prosper and thrive when promises are kept, even the little commitments like taking out the trash are honored.

4. Procrastination delays or prevents any improvement in your relationship. Weeks or months with no change brings the situation to a head or a crisis. Healthy resolution requires eliminating procrastination, which you think you might do - tomorrow.

See where we're going here? No relationship, personal or professional, can survive the sabotage of procrastination. Something cracks the relationship wide open and most often it ends in failure to resolve. The sad fact is noteworthy: your self-esteem takes larger and larger hits until a self-perpetuating cycle emerges of broken relationships and broken partnerships.

The hopeful thing is that this is something you can change. You can repair a damaged relationship by simply *not* procrastinating. You can rebuild trust. All you need is a repair of your crossed wires. In the daily hacks, we're going to tackle the job head-on.

Mindset

One of the biggest casualties in the destructive cycle of procrastination is *you*, my friend. The consistent habit of putting things off affects your day-to-day life and initiates a habit you find hard to break. The mindset is destructive in every aspect of your life:

- Loss of time: Time slips away when you engage in momentary pleasures over meeting life's goals. Squandered moments represent a loss of the one commodity you can never replace.
- Blown opportunities: Opportunity knocks, but how often? Some pivotal breaks make or break your career. The impact on you and your relationships is enormous.

- Ruined career: Procrastination can lose you your job. The loss of income doesn't affect only you. Your companion or roommate or family bear the brunt of the loss of wages. You stand to lose more than your career.

- Ruined options: When you squander your time, you end up taking shortcuts and making poor choices. Because you put things off, you have fewer, not more options available to you.

- Damaged reputation: You become *that* person. *That* person no one wants on the team. *That* person no one wants on the trip. *That* person you don't even like.

Naturally, your self-esteem drops and drops and hits rock bottom. Worse, you don't see change anywhere in sight. It's time to turn that around by engaging in the 31 days of life hacks; it's time to rewire your brain.

The long term effects of procrastination cripple your life and create a downward spiral you feel like you can't change. That's the myth, my friend. Inside of you remains a kernel of hope, a glimmer of understanding. You weren't born this way. You were made this way, and you can be unmade. You can change. Yes, you can.

First, name the problem. Be honest and real. I think you're here.

Second, take baby steps. The 31 life hacks represent a month of daily activities.

Third, put it into practice. Take action with what you learn for the next 31 days.

Part II:
Life Hacks to Conquer Procrastination

The next 31 daily headlines are designed for your meaningful participation. The first eight focus on the negative behaviors motivating your procrastination. *I call it slaying the giants because each of these next eight topics loom over you, larger than life.* In each one, we will explore how to conquer it and you will choose an exercise to eradicate that giant from your life.

Day One: Fear of Failure

Tracy had a love/hate relationship with laundry. Well, okay, mostly hate. The never-ending aspect of always more loads to run, fold and put away made coming home from work depressing. She always began with sorting through the mail. She then emptied the dishwasher and started supper. She picked up strewn backpacks and ensured the children were doing their homework. By the time dinner ended and the kids were in bed, she was drained. Laundry was the absolute last thing on her mind.

"Mom, I don't have any clean underwear for tomorrow," one hollered from her bedroom.

"Aren't you supposed to be in bed?"

"Um, yes. But I wanted to set out my clothes for tomorrow. I have to give an oral presentation. I want to be sure I have just the right outfit. That's when I realized I'm out of clean underwear."

"I'll take care of it," she sighed. One single load of whites got done. The scenario is repeated the next night when yet another emergency arose. Why did Tracy procrastinate doing laundry? It isn't a high-tech job. There was no fear of failure or was there? Tracy is a single mom since divorcing her cheating ex. His snide comments echoed in her subconscious (and her conscious mind as well) every time she walked in the door. "You won't be able to manage without me." "You'll be begging me to come back." Yes, her fear of failure hovered over every evening.

Step One: Ponder

How much does fear of failure loom over you and cause you to procrastinate about an assignment? Here's how to tell:

- Failing makes you worry about what other people think about you. Their opinion matters and actually colors your own: *Am I a fraud after all?*
- Failing casts a shadow over the future you want more than anything else. Rather than destroy the hope of the future, you resist any action that might cause it to disappear.
- Failing makes you worry others will lose interest in you. You will no longer be a bright prospect. You will no longer be attractive. Subconsciously, you seek to postpone that possible judgment, no matter the cost.
- Failing might cause the people you value most to feel a genuine disappointment in

you. You owe them so much and can't bear the thought of letting them down.

- Failing makes you see how unprepared, uneducated, incapable you really are. You can feel the illusion of control slipping away.

- Failure can be avoided if you offer disclaimers. "Don't expect too much." "I didn't have time." Procrastination is a defense mechanism with built-in alibis.

- Failing is the realization that you played your highest card and you have nothing more to offer.

- Fear of failure produces somatic complaints like headaches, stomachaches or other symptoms to prevent you from beginning and thus failing.

- Fear of failure is avoided by letting distractions pull you away from the assigned task. You didn't fail, you got ambushed by a competing priority.

Does any of this ring true for you? If you identify with even a third of these indicators, your procrastination is partially derived from a fear of failure. Postponement long ago became a defense mechanism for averting disaster, and you've been employing it ever since. This represents a crossed wire and our job now is to rewire the mechanism.

Step Two: Write

Don't try to finish all these writing exercises at once. Do one today. If this is a significant issue for you, revisit the topic multiple times. Short-circuited wires need time to form new synapses and the more you send your life's current along these newly formed paths, the stronger the pathway becomes. There is no fear of failure when you realize there is no wrong answer, no preconceived idea of what you will accomplish, no grade. Expect gut wrenching progress as you write your way to success.

❖ Where does your fear of failure come from? Write about a time you failed, how you felt, what happened. Realize you did the best you could. Winston Churchill, that giant breathing hope on London during the World War II blitz, said, "Success is stumbling from failure to failure with no loss of enthusiasm." His life was punctuated by many political defeats but that never defined him. What definition would you want for your life?

❖ To what extent did your parents instil a fear of failure in you? Were they always demanding the best of you? Excessively high expectations affect us throughout life. Write about your parent's disappointment over a grade or event and how you felt. Identify factors beyond your control. Identify limits of age and experience. Were their expectations realistic? Realize you did the best you could. Write what you'd have loved them to have said instead.

❖ To what extent are you a fly caught in the web of past failures? Write about a time when you felt like a failure but in looking back as an outsider, it's now clear you had nothing to do with the outcome. You were present, but you were not the determining factor. You see famous people and forget their paths to glory were marred by many failures along the way. Marilyn Monroe once said, "Just because you fail once doesn't mean you're gonna fail at everything." Give yourself some grace.

❖ How could you simplify a task before you to make it more achievable? If you can put it into bite-sized tidbits, cut through to the heart of the challenge or in some way make it easier, would you begin? Consider fulfilling half of the task or asking for help or rewriting the challenge into something you believe you can accomplish. Take a current challenge you are avoiding and implement one of these coping techniques.

❖ Learn to set realistic expectations for yourself. Define what really constitutes failure. What outcome would be satisfactory in your mind? Think of a task currently assigned to you. Perhaps it's a task you've been avoiding, one you feel might be too much for you. List two realistic expectations. For example, as opposed to getting an A, realize a B is still above average. If you feel like a promotion is riding on this project, lower your expectation of the outcome. You will advance when the time is right: if not now, soon. It's okay to finish and not be spectacular. How does the following quote affect your expectations for yourself?

"We expect more of ourselves than we have any right to."
Oliver Wendall Holmes

Step 3: Visualize

End today's writing exercise by visualizing what it would look like to begin a project or task without fear of failure. Imagine all your friends cheering for you as the gun is set to signal the start of the race, and you embrace the outcome rather than fear it.

Step 4: Set Goals

What do you want to accomplish?

Where do you want to be in one month?

What challenge do you want to conquer today?

What is a reasonable time frame for feeling no fear of failure?

Day Two: Fear of Asking for Help

"Don't be afraid to ask questions. Don't be afraid to ask for help when you need it. I do that every day. Asking for help isn't a sign of weakness; it's a sign of strength. It shows you have the courage to admit when you don't know something, and to learn something new."
Barack Obama

Tim wanted more than anything else to be on the debate team. The only problem? He was afraid to speak in public. His current flame, Jenny, always commented on how cool the geeks were in their suits spewing their suave presentations.

"Give me a wrench and a carburetor and I can impress anyone. But put me in front of people with a script? I'm a walking idiot," he muttered after one such exchange.

"Why don't you talk to the speech teacher?" Jenny meant to be helpful.

"Why don't you mind your own business?" Tim snapped back. Tim had never asked for help since the day he asked his dad a question about changing the oil. He'd been twelve. Did his dad appreciate his son's precocious interest in mechanics? No. His father's response was, "You don't know that? How many times have you watched me change the oil? You need to open your eyes, bud."

He felt like such a fool that he vowed to never ask anyone for help again. Ever.

Step One: Ponder

You've been given an assignment. It's important. Then it hits you: You don't know exactly how to proceed. You're feeling it in the pit of your stomach. Sound familiar? You're suffering from fear of asking for help. Don't hit the panic button quite yet. This is a common predicament and learning curves are part of the process.

It's true. No successful person, either in sports, on the stage or in business achieved success without receiving a little help. Talent is not the key to success. Success comes with overcoming your fear of asking for help.

Deeply rooted in this giant is the perceived weakness in asking questions. Like a by-product of an age-old maxim, *real men don't cry,* the idea that top achievers never ask for help is simply a myth. Dispel the notion that your questions make you a burden to others.

If you are hesitant to ask for help in the workplace, think again: Realize that your questions will often clarify the thoughts of others. Your questions may be the linchpin in the cog of success for the whole team. No matter how often you feel like you are interrupting another person's flow of work, the team needs to have it done right the first time around. Your co-worker will feel like asking for help is a sign of respect.

If you are a student asking for help, adjust your expectations: Realize your instructor asked a million questions in achieving his/her own station in life. Instructors appreciate your interest. If it was expected that you already knew everything about the subject, there would be no point in teaching the class.

Asking for clarification is never wrong, either in the classroom or the workplace. No one can succeed if the objective remains unclear. Keep these hints in mind in preparation for approaching an instructor, a boss or a colleague:

1. Ask the right questions. In trying to figure out the problem, what have you considered thus far? Write it down. Clarify your thoughts. Make a list of your questions as succinctly as possible.
2. Study how others ask for help. Especially in the workplace, someone knows how to approach the boss. Observe how it's done or ask a colleague for tips on how/when the boss is most approachable. Ask them, "What is the best way to ask for help on this project?"
3. Find a mentor. In every circle of contact, someone knows the answer. That someone will feel honored when asked to take you

under his/her wing. Rehearse the wording. Find the right time. Ask. "I admire your work. I'd appreciate being able to search your brain on _______." Be specific. You aren't asking for an inordinate amount of hand-holding forever. You are asking for an answer to a specific question.

The important thing is to move past your fear by realizing the benefits of asking for help. *There are a lot of good reasons for reaching out.*

Step Two: Write

❖ Not asking for help sends the wrong message. Your boss or instructor may be waiting for you to ask for clarification. Your reluctance may come across as low self-esteem or arrogance. Write down how you want to be perceived, and then write a question that reflects your goal. How do these words from Brene Brown reflect your place in the world?

"One of the greatest barriers to connection is the cultural importance we place on 'going it alone.' Somehow we've come to equate success with not needing anyone. Many of us are willing to extend a helping hand, but we're very reluctant to reach out for help when we need it ourselves. It's as if we've divided the world into 'those who offer help' and 'those who need help.' The truth is that we are both."
Brene Brown

❖ Think of a looming assignment. Write down your ideas. List what you know. Think through the outcomes. When you ask for input, you want to be perceived as thoughtful, so distill this information into a specific query. How does this quote from Chris Rock affect your reasoning?

"I used to have horrible cars that would always end up broken down on the highway. When I tried to flag someone down, nobody stopped. But if I pushed my own car, other drivers would get out and push with me. If you want help, help yourself - people like to see that."
Chris Rock

❖ Rehearse your question. Be prepared to ask a well-worded question without rambling, long explanations and going off on a tangent. Respect the person's time constraints. Write out your question and then practice in front of a mirror. Learn to see your question as a thoughtful, respected contribution. Cesar Chavez is quoted as saying, "You are never so strong that you don't need help." Do you believe this quote is true? Why?

❖ Turn to a mentor before a boss. Someone else has been in your shoes and in your place before. Finding that person and cultivating a relationship helps you tackle the tough jobs. List people who might fit the bill. Write out a way to approach one of them. Oprah Winfrey put it well: "A mentor is someone who allows you to see the hope inside yourself." Who might that be for you?

❖ If you need help dealing with a fellow student or colleague, deal face-to-face before involving an instructor or boss. Learning how to handle interpersonal conflict is a skill you will need throughout life. Write a short paragraph about a current or recent conflict. What could you honestly say? Don't apologize for anything you don't feel is your fault. The idea is to undo rather than add to the situation. That's a great beginning: "I'm sorry there is tension between us and I'd love to resolve this misunderstanding."

❖ Rewire the whole idea of *asking for help* by learning to reword it. Think of this as gathering data or the process of collaboration or seeking confirmation. Make a list of all the ways *asking for help* could be reworded. Realize that in all hero tales, the hero asks for help. J.R.R. Tolkien's Mithrandir said, "And help oft shall come from the hands of the weak when the Wise falter." Help comes with an invitation.

Step 3: Visualize

End today's writing exercise by visualizing yourself asking for help. Who would you ask? What would you wear? Where would you plan to be when making the request?

Step 4: Set Goals

What do you want to accomplish?

Where do you want to be in one month?

What challenge do you want to conquer today?

What is a reasonable time frame for feeling no

fear of asking for help?

Day Three: Perfectionism

You know you aren't Superman. Still, you expect yourself to get things right. *If I turn in this report and I've missed something important, there goes my raise!* The request for information has been sitting on your desk for three days now. You know you should finish it but, every time you look at it, sweat breaks out on your forehead and you immediately see another more urgent task.

Logic doesn't enter into the equation. Neither does respect for time. The only thing you can think about is how important the report is, and how perfect it's got to be. Tomorrow, you'll finally be ready to tackle it. Who are you fooling? Tomorrow you'll still be wondering, *Is it good enough? Am I good enough?*

Step One: Ponder

It is infinitely harder to start a project if the first draft has to be perfect. When I begin writing a book, I always go back to the words of one of my favorite authors. She doesn't know me but she has been my vicarious mentor for many years.

"Perfectionism is the voice of the oppressor, the enemy of the people. It will keep you cramped and insane your whole life, and it is the main obstacle between you and a shitty first draft."
Anne Lamott

It's true. Your inner critic works overtime when you begin a task and, if left unchecked, runs amok. Somewhere in your past you did well and a crazy loop of endless perfection became your dictator for life. It's time to uncross those wires. You are living your life in a plane of negativity, expecting love and approval for a job well done rather than for being yourself. The tendency has made you into a person who procrastinates simply because you might not be perfect. Let's be real. There is a chasm between striving for excellence and demanding perfection from yourself.

Let's look at two ways in which this unhealthy cycle manifests itself. The first is self-imposed. You are hooked on the praise of others and, if you can't get it, the assignment isn't worth doing. The second is societal. The perfect pictures on Facebook, the self-adulation of public figures and the excessive salaries paid to stars and studs all give the illusion that society knows best. The message is that if you fulfill society's penchant for dress and behavior, you will be perfect. Nope. Not even close. A healthy sense of self comes from acceptance of self.

Underlying the whole quest for perfection is a competition forced upon many of us from birth: get into the right preschool, make the highest grade, get accepted on the team, look like everyone else. Social media exacerbates the impossibly high standards. Here's the tragedy: even if you succeed and attain perfection in some area of your life, you will remain unhappy. You will remain self-critical, always raising the bar on yourself. Do it a little faster. Do it a little better. Be a little more.

So are you a perfectionist or a person who likes to stand out, a high achiever? Look at these tell-tale signs of perfectionists:

- All-or-nothing thinking. Being almost perfect is a failure.
- Having a push versus pull mentality. It is healthy to be pulled toward a goal, but a perfectionist has to be pushed to get work

done. Postponing the task leaves the illusion of perfection intact.

- Having a critical eye. You find every little mistake and tend to focus on imperfections. Admit it, you're looking for spelling errors or the errant dangling participle as you read this book.
- Setting unrealistic standards. You want to be the best at everything, even if it's something you're not interested in.
- Emphasis on results. Most of us like the challenge of creating or building something grand. A perfectionist only likes the finished product of the highest ideal.
- You are your own worst and harshest critic.
- You are defensive when criticized.
- You look forward to the destination, never enjoying the journey.

If any of these characteristics resonate with you, you are confirming what you already know. You don't just like to do a good job, you expect all your work to be pretty darn near perfect. Rewiring your brain requires the shift in understanding that perfect is the enemy of good. Learning to accept good work is the challenge before you. But realize your misguided goal here.

"Perfect is not a quest for the best. It is the pursuit of the worst in ourselves, the part that tells us that nothing we do will ever be good enough, that we should try harder."
Julia Cameron

Step Two: Write

You will need to come back to these exercises a number of times to consistently rewire your brain to accept a job well done in place of the ridiculously high standard of perfection. That's okay. Time is on your side.

❖ Write down your strengths and recognize that setbacks are an expected part of life. What does that look like? For each strength in your list, put a dash and follow it up with a short description of a normal setback. Now translate that to a current project. What is your ideal? What is reasonable?

❖ Rather than focusing on self-defeating thoughts, find the positive in your faults. List some of your imperfections. Now, extrapolate a positive aspect for each one. Remove terms like "never" or "always." Give yourself grace. How does this quote color your thinking?

❖ Part of your rewire is learning to set realistic goals you can actually achieve. Draw a line down the center of the page. On the left side: Think of a project and list grandiose goals that make you a superstar. On the right side rewrite each goal for a normal person. See the difference?

"Embrace being perfectly imperfect.
Learn from your mistakes and forgive yourself,
you'll be happier."
Roy Bennet

❖ Learn to break a large, overwhelming assignment into smaller bites you can accomplish more easily. Read the quote below and decide if it's true. Either way, break a large goal down into smaller pieces and see what they look like. When you dream smaller dreams, there is more of a chance you'll actually take action. Meeting small goals gives you the confidence to move on to bigger goals. If life is a marathon and not a sprint, let yourself run one leg at a time.

❖ Work on developing a laser focus on one actionable item at a time. Alexander Graham Bell said, "The sun's rays do not burn until brought to a focus." This was long before the advent of laser beams, and the age old truth remains. Write down one broad goal or assignment. Now, distill *one actionable item* from this to accomplish today. Laser beams can cut as thin a slice as 15 microns. So how would a laser focus allow you to accomplish something today?

❖ Turn mistakes into learning situations. Think of a mistake you've made on an assignment or project. What lessons can you glean from that experience? How can those lessons keep you from making the same mistake again?

"Smart people do stupid things. Stupid people don't learn from them."
Frank Sonnenberg

Step 3: Visualize

End today's writing exercise by granting yourself the freedom to be less than perfect. What would that look like? Analyze if your perfectionism makes you a happier or more productive person. Visualize the way you want to feel.

Step 4: Set Goals

What do you want to accomplish?

Where do you want to be in one month?

What challenge do you want to conquer today?

What is a reasonable time frame for feeling no fear of perfection?

Day Four: Self-Doubt

"When you doubt your power, you give power to your doubt."
Honore de Balzac

Step One: Ponder

Are you an over-thinker? Do you make decisions and then get caught in a destructive loop of rethinking and reanalyzing them? Being riddled with self-doubt requires a rewiring of your brain. Often, self-doubt begins in early childhood when your parents tell you that your feelings or thoughts or actions are wrong. When you hear this all the time, you begin to doubt yourself. You question yourself constantly: Is every thought, every word, every action a mistake?

Closely tied to low self-esteem, self-doubt manifests itself in several ways. You can spot this tendency in yourself if you hate to give yourself any credit. You probably heard disparaging comments like, "Don't be getting a big head" or, "No one likes a braggart." Belittling throughout childhood leads to an adulthood of excessive self doubt.

Another way to spot this tendency is if you recognize the imposter syndrome as a part of your makeup. Do you secretly feel like one day you'll be the proverbial emperor with no clothes, called out as a fraud? You feel like your awards, your titles, your grades, your position is somehow a fluke, a mistake; if everyone knew the *real* you, everything would vanish in a puff of smoke. You didn't really deserve any of it. This is especially common among young professional women who rose in the workforce amid conflicting expectations of it being a man's world and their need to overcompensate to get noticed.

Look at the six descriptions that are symptomatic of self-doubt:

1. You have trouble accepting praise. (You don't deserve compliments.)
2. You are known as a workaholic. (You loop energy into a good project.)
3. You are driven to do your best. (You'd rather be a big fish in a small sea.)
4. You are described as being a perfectionist by others. (You, therefore, must always be perfect.)
5. You are paralyzed by a fear of failure. (It is not an option.)
6. You think you're lucky or charming but never accomplished.

If you see yourself in these descriptions, your psyche is layered with wires reinforcing all the wrong patterns.

Self-doubt is a poison corroding the wires in your brain. Left unchecked, it will eventually shatter you from within. In essence, you are the enemy destroying yourself. Your basic life essence, the source of your internal strength and power, comes into question a hundred times a day and the poison spreads.

Your self-doubt is sabotaging your success by looping endless self-fulfilling thoughts about each step you undertake. No one is telling you that your ideas are stupid: you are. No one is criticizing your work: you are. Your inner critic, your self-doubt is the enemy of success.

Research bears this out. A study of more than 600 high school students revealed proof that a self-doubt loop is the only limitation of your ability to achieve your goals. Students were told one of three statements:

1. Your IQ is fixed. It cannot be changed.
2. Rare cases of increasing the IQ have occurred, but that is very rare indeed.
3. Your IQ fluctuates and does not predict how smart you'll be a year from now.

The results were revelatory. Students who believed they could become smarter got better grades and accomplished more. The other two groups performed poorly, reinforcing their own self-doubt.

Forget motivational talks. Pep talks will not change you. What will? Action. Taking action that creates a change in attitude removes self-doubt.

Step Two: Write

❖ Write down an assignment you've been procrastinating about. If you doubt you can do it, acknowledge those feelings. Next, write down all the evidence showing that you deserve your place at the table. Write down past successes and validating commendations. There is power in seeing this on paper. Realize your past for what it truly is. The strongest method for eliminating self-doubt is dispelling the untruth at its basis.

❖ Afford yourself the grace you extend to others: Give yourself a second chance. Write down the mindset you want, and let this be a new beginning. Now write down a task you've been procrastinating on. Imagine how a confident person would approach the assignment. You are that person. Write down one actionable item. Do it.

❖ Learn to stop it in its tracks. Name one self-doubt you have about a current assignment. Now disrupt that loop by writing down proof you can succeed. The process of setting boundaries for your own mind empowers you to stop the self-doubt spiral.

❖ Build belief in yourself. Like John and Michael in Peter Pan, they had to believe in pixie dust to be able to fly. You have to believe in the magical pixie dust in your own life as well. Write down one success that led to being given this assignment. You passed a qualifying class, you earned a degree, you did well on a prior assignment. Something led you to where you are today. That trail of accomplishments is your power. Post this list where you can read it every day. Like all the

Lost Boys, you have to believe in yourself to accomplish your best. Create the self-fulfilling prophecy of success, not the death-spiral of self-doubt.

❖ Build on steps. Celebrate the accomplishment of achieving small goals and individual steps in achieving this project. These celebrations of yourself begin the process of strengthening the rewiring of your brain. By now you should recognize the following quote to be true. Write down one good step you've taken and how to celebrate that accomplishment.

"Our doubts are traitors, and make us lose the good we oft might win, by fearing to attempt."
William Shakespeare

❖ Take yourself out of center stage. One way to eliminate self-doubt is to eliminate the need to be great. The world around you is so busy acting in their own life's dramas, they aren't watching your every move. By shifting your focus, you can shift the importance of each thing you do. You can start that project fixing the bathroom floor because no one cares how great it looks. Write down the first steps to start a project you've been procrastinating and list some *good enough* parameters. Take those steps.

Step Three: Visualize

If you want to be a confident version of yourself, learn to see yourself as one.

Step 4: Set Goals

Where do you want to be in one month?

What does your image of yourself look like today?

What is a reasonable time frame for undoing all this self-doubt?

Day Five: Exaggerated Optimism

"I always like to look on the optimistic side of life,but I am realistic enough to know that life is a complex matter."
Walt Disney

Step One: Ponder

In contrast to the death spiral of self-doubt rests another negative component of procrastination. "Easy peasy! I can whip this out in no time!" "I'll do this later. Right now I want to do something completely different." If you recognize either of those statements as words you've uttered, you might be suffering from a sense of exaggerated optimism. You don't see yourself as arrogant or foolhardy, you just think it's not that big a deal. Your mindset causes you to procrastinate; in the process, you set yourself up for failure. That failure can affect others around you.

This isn't as uncommon as you think, and it has earned different names as psychologists have tried to understand it. Some have called it the Victory Disease. A classic example is the defeat of Xerxes in the Greco-Persia war in 480 BC. Because of superior numbers, Xerxes expected an easy victory. Because the Greeks utilized a smarter strategy, they defeated the larger empire. Xerxes was defeated by his own exaggerated confidence.

Others psychologists labelled it the Stockdale Paradox after the Vietnam War in the 1960's. As one of the longest POWs held in captivity, James Stockdale was described as someone who consistently believed in being rescued by Christmas. He held this belief so strongly and so optimistically that he became depressed when it failed to happen. Realistic views led to a higher survival rate among the prison population.

The impact of exaggerated optimism has caused faulty wiring inside your brain. Consider these consequences:

1. You lie to yourself and if you continue in the behavior, your brain creates unrealistic loops that make the behavior a habit.
2. Your focus gets locked into one aspect of the assignment to the exclusion of all others.
3. Your wrong concept of reality causes you to move in the wrong direction.
4. Your false sense of security eliminates your need for a fail-safe option when it goes sideways.
5. You develop the destructive habit of basing your actions on a perverted sense of reality.

The problem with overestimating your abilities is the eventual loss of money, status, trust or position when you fail to deliver. Often you will not realize your mistake until it is too late to recover. There are things you can do, however, to avoid the collision of perception with reality.

Step Two: Write

❖ Get feedback. Make sure you understand the task or assignment. Write it out in your own words and ask for clarification. Is it really as simple as it looks? Have you overlooked necessary research? Choose something you've been procrastinating because it looks like it won't take that long and fulfill this step.

❖ Time block the assignment. Writing it into your planner forces you to make time for it rather than postponing it until the last minute. Create a time buffer ensuring success.

* Get your creative juices going by brainstorming all the things you *don't* know about the project. This reality check forces your brain to acknowledge what needs to be done.

* Develop a realistic version of optimism. What you need isn't a dose of positive thinking, it's a dose of reality. Real optimism sees the pitfalls in the assignment and knows how long it will take and sees the bright side of reality. A self-deluded optimist only sees the outcome. Think of an assignment or task you've been procrastinating because its completion won't take long. Now list all the things that could go wrong. Do you see the difference?

Step Three: Visualize

Learn to see what is real. Visualize an easy assignment as a test of character. Will you tackle it and acknowledge its value or do you see it as an unworthy opponent? Visualize arming yourself with honesty, reality and perseverance.

Step 4: Set Goals

Where do you want to be in one month?

What does your image of yourself look like today?

What is a reasonable time frame for overcoming this false view of reality?

Day Six: Worry

"When I look back on all these worries, I remember the story of the old man who said on his deathbed that he had had a lot of trouble in his life, most of which had never happened."
Winston Churchill

Step One: Ponder

Worry is easy to understand. It's that nagging queasy stomach, that anxious dread that keeps us awake at night, that tightening of the jaw or grinding of the teeth that makes us dread starting when we should. It's a leading cause of procrastination. In a society bombarded by stress, adding *one more thing* causes us to reach a tipping point. We can't. We don't.

Procrastinators fail to act because of their overall anxiety levels. To cure procrastination, we must begin to reduce the worry overload. We must uncross the wire pathways built up over time and establish a healthier mindset.

While everyone worries from time to time, some chronic worriers grew up in reverse parenting homes where they assumed too much responsibility at a young age. The result was a burden of care, which translated into worry, and it became a pattern for life.

Situational worry causes anxiety overloads. You have too much on your plate. every. single. day. You are overwhelmed: Place to-do reminders into slots where you can forget about them now and pick them up at the appropriate moment.

The worry of uncertainty stems from having so much out of your control. You don't know if you have a free day next Tuesday because the school sends home late announcements. You don't know if you can handle another to-do because it's complicated by childcare issues. You get stuck working through every possible scenario caused by not knowing what to expect. You must set limits. You can also time block various types of commitments into your schedule. You don't know what they are yet, but you can see your available time periods for getting an assignment done.

Reduce your overall worry load by taking action, physical action. The Mayo Clinic cites physical exercise as an antidote to worry because it increases endorphins, improves mood and serves as a way to meditate subconsciously as we use those big muscles.

Improve your lifestyle. Drink more water. Eat nutritious meals. Cut out the junk. Go to bed on time. These significant steps keep your anxiety levels within bounds and through them you exercise a measure of control over your life.

Learn to live in the moment. Worry robs us of the present, painting an unreal landscape of the future. Slow down. Force yourself to take your time in each activity; by doing so, you learn to focus on the present. If worry threatens to overwhelm you, stop. Reconnect with the present by listening to the sounds around you. Smell the air. Look at life in front of you. By steadfastly rejecting that future landscape, you rewire your brain into a present healthy mindset.

Cultivate an attitude of gratitude. By learning to consciously appreciate your life, you reduce worry and develop a healthy life and a healthy mind. Contentment improves your sleep at night, ultimately making the rewiring process easier.

Once you start to get a handle on your worry overload, you can more effectively deal with the procrastination that stems from worry over an assignment. Let's address things you can do when you procrastinate and start the rewiring process.

Step Two: Write

❖ Get your worry about a task out of the dark recesses of your mind and onto paper in the cleansing rays of broad daylight. Write down an assignment or project you are worried about. Now identify three factors causing your worry. Writing them out brings ideas for solving potential problems. Write those solutions down as well.

❖ Make a choice. Julia Cameron feeds affirmations to a worried soul. Here are some I've found helpful:

- Leap and the net will appear.
- Survival lies in sanity, and sanity lies in paying attention.
- Wherever you are is always the right place. There is never a need to fix anything, to hitch up the bootstraps of the soul and start at some higher place. Start right where you are.

Write down a favorite affirmation and highlight it with a red colored pencil. Add other affirmations as you find them, and highlight them as well. A little self medication goes a long way.

- Practice action-focused journaling. Write down a project you aren't quite ready to start, one you are worried about. Now write down the worst possible outcome. What would you do if that happened? Write down the best possible outcome if you started right in. What is one thing you can do right now to ensure that best possible outcome?

- Journaling your worry about a project has several benefits. These include helping you clarify your thoughts, reviewing your past experience, reflection about your feelings, understanding your emotions and release of negative thoughts. Which of these do you find most helpful? Choose a project to write about, and then decide which of these benefits were derived from the experience.
- Write down an assignment in detail. Define the scope. List the steps to completion. Analyze options. As you wrote, identify when you felt that worry dissipate. Which step helped the most? Good to know, isn't it?

Step Three: Visualize

What would your life look like with less stress? Would it change your appearance? Would it change your facial expression? Would it change the things you do? Imagine your life with fifty percent less stress, and make this your goal. Lose fifty pounds of worry.

Step four: Set Goals

Where do you want to be in one month?

What does your life look like with less stress?

What is a reasonable time frame for reducing physical symptoms of stress?

Day Seven: Boredom

"Boredom can be a lethal thing on a small island."
Christopher Moore

Mundane routines and endless days without a break -- we've all been there. In that subversive land of boredom, some of the most important roadblocks to productivity creep into view. Indeed, the negative effects of boredom include substance abuse, depression, anxiety, poor academic performance, increased addiction to taking risks and aggressive behaviors.

Do we pick up the phone and start scrolling through Facebook because we are bored or does our addition to social media serve as the reason all else bores us? Psychologists like to debate the cause and effect of the cycle, but this much is true: we need stimulation because we are bored and, when the activity ends, a higher dose of stimulation is required to keep the cycle going. This increasing need for stimulation and the resulting lows of boredom set up a repetitive cycle leading to the wires in our brains getting short circuited.

On a day when time drags and we feel like the boredom is killing us, it may be true. Boredom leads to compulsive eating, less exercise and increased stress. The toll is measured by indicators like obesity, hypertension and heart disease. Yes, boredom kills.

It is important to realize what boredom really is - - sadness. The opposite of happiness is not unhappiness. Its opposite is the ennui of having no feeling at all: boredom. Recognizing your sadness is one important element in trying to cure boredom when it is the cause of your procrastination. At the root, it is an issue of control.

Boredom results when you have no control over the situation. You are forced to wait in a doctor's office. You must sit and listen to an instructor droning on and on. You have to balance the checkbook and pay the bills when you already know there isn't enough money for anything you'd *like* to be doing. In most instances of life, we take control and change the situation. We close the boring book. We change the channel in the middle of a boring program. Boredom results when we are no longer free to take control.

I was forced to read Dosteovsky's *Crime and Punishment* in school. I found the sentence structure convoluted and the theme mind-killing. I never touched anything else by Dosteovsky, or any other Russian author, either. I was also assigned *Pride and Prejudice*. The class discussions made the novel so interesting, I read it over and over again. I read every Austen and Bronte book I could check out from the library. Boredom changed me.

When you begin to associate certain tasks or assignments as *boring*, you build a pattern of resistance that can affect you as well as others. Boredom in driving down a freeway leads the driver to seek distraction, and an accident ensues. Consider the scale when the bored person is an air traffic controller.

The negativity of these forced excursions into the wasteland of boredom and the subsequent need for greater and greater stimulus can affect you forever, unless you take specific action to get those wires uncrossed.

Step Two: Write

- ❖ What boring task or assignment lies waiting for your attention? Implement a short fifteen minute burst of activity to get it started. For example, you may be dreading an hour of working out at the gym. A 15 minute burst to get your duffle bag in the car and start toward the gym impels you to finish the activity. Who drives to the gym, walks in and then leaves? Most of us go ahead and exercise. Write about this and what you learned about yourself.

- ❖ Give Future You a chance. You've been putting something off because you think it's a bore, because you don't think you'll ever be glad you did it. Get acquainted with what Future You might say. Write a memory you might have two days or a week from now, if you started that boring project today.

❖ Send Future You an email. I'm serious as a heart attack. Go to FutureMe.org and send yourself an email, to be delivered on any day you pick. Tell your future self how bored you are and how you're tackling the dreaded project anyway. When it's due and you get the email, see how you feel. Instead of feeling negative about what you *have* to do, you will start feeling *grateful* for doing it now. It works.

❖ Reward each step of progress. Boredom results from lack of directed attention. Write down a task or assignment you've been postponing. List the value of getting it done. What would make it easier? I love dark chocolate-covered espresso beans. I get one for each step I complete as I plow through a boring, dreaded task. I also like to keep a list of those rewards in my journal.

❖ Plan ahead. When you block out your schedule, you ensure a mix of engaging and mind-numbing activities. You end up remaining productive and map out your time so each mundane task is rewarded with something much more rewarding. Make a list of tasks to schedule.

❖ Pair what you expect to be boring with what you know to be compelling. Listen to an audio book or a podcast while you pay the bills. Then write down three things you learned. You may have tricked yourself into getting the job done but the more often you do this, the more you strengthen the connections that foster productivity.

❖ To coin a Star Trek phrase, *Resistance is Futile*. You must do certain mundane tasks. They will not disappear. No one is going to do your mundane tasks as well as their own, so accept it. Remind yourself of three good things you love about your life, and then do the task you've been avoiding. Write the three things down in case you don't remember them tomorrow.

Step Three: Visualize

What would your life look like if everything got done on time? Imagine your life as a model of productivity.

Step four: Set Goals

Where do you want to be in one month?

What three things can you do to alleviate boredom?

What is a reasonable time frame for eliminating the thought *I'm bored* from your vocabulary?

Day Eight: Conflict Avoidance

Step one: Ponder

There is nothing psychiatrists love more than a healthy discussion over conflict avoidance. Constructs of desire and avoidance can be distilled down to how much you want to achieve something versus how much you want to suffer the consequences for avoiding the same something. Pretty straightforward, isn't it? Guess again.

It's actually riddled with all kinds of subsets of behaviors tucked into the recesses of your mind, behaviors you probably aren't aware of, stemming from motivations you have to dig to discover. Let's look at the most common subset. Find what resonates with you and you'll be halfway to figuring out how to uncross your wires.

The key is digging deep and being brutally honest with yourself, because self-deception is the basis for most of these crossed wires.

"A great deal of intelligence can be invested in ignorance when the need for illusion is deep."
Saul Bellow

The typical conflict avoidance personality runs from a fight. Any fight at all. Our household is a prime example. A husband, mother, three children. Let one person explode in frustration, and suddenly the room is empty as everyone hides in their room until the storm has passed. We're just not fighters by nature.

What are specific signs that you fall into this category? Are you a people pleaser? Do you deflect conflict with a joke or a distraction? Do you stockpile grievances and let them out in a burst of emotion? These are sure signs you've been avoiding conflict for some time. You may have a history of childhood trauma where conflict wounded your soul. Most of all, what lengths will you go to in order to avoid a conflict? Inveterate avoiders will suffer injustice and let others trample over them to prevent conflict. If you're dealing with another turtle who hides in its shell, instead of healthy discussion, there is often an elephant in the room. Is this you?

If you find yourself behind the magic eight ball of this page, you procrastinate because the task at hand creates a conflict for you. What do you do with conflict? You escape. You delay. You procrastinate.

There are consequences for remaining in this uncomfortable place. Suppressing emotions leads to physical manifestations. It instills in your psyche an element of fear; in avoiding what seems unsafe over and over again, you build loops of crossed wires. You end up with a lot of regrets, a lot of missed opportunities when a simple resolution might have cleared up misunderstandings, and the conflict might have become a source of pleasure.

How might this look in real life? Jean is late for an appointment, circling the parking lot for an empty spot. Ah! She sees one. She looks apprehensively at the dashboard clock. She has less than five minutes to park, enter the building and find the right office. She pulls in, turns off the motor, puts the keys in her pocket and leaves the car. As she starts to walk away, another driver yells, "Lady, where did you learn to park?" Horrified, she turns and sees her car is indeed crooked between the lines, close to another vehicle. Here are Jean's options:

- She could say nothing and walk away (avoiding all conflict).
- She could apologize and walk away (avoiding all conflict).
- She could yell back, "Deal with it!" (aggressive).
- She could calmly point out the other drivers have ample room (assertive).

The key to rewiring your brain lies in option number four, learning to be assertive. When you can tackle issues head on, you can figure out why you are procrastinating a certain task, assignment or project and then be assertive with yourself.

You can develop a better way of handling conflict.

1. Be honest with yourself. What are you feeling? Recognize it and set it aside.

2. Look at the situation. What is the other's position and what is yours?

3. Come up with exactly the right words to say.

4. Speak your mind calmly and respectfully.

Practice this in easy situations, and develop a degree of comfort in the process. It becomes a new healthy habit the more you do it.

Step two: Write

Choose from these writing prompts and come back to them if you need to. If you chronically avoid conflict, it will take some practice to wire your brain for healthy conflict resolution.

❖ Look at a task you typically avoid. Write it out, and write out what bugs you about it. Be specific. Now write down this question: What will happen if I don't do this promptly? Shift your focus from not wanting to do something, to instead dwell on the negative aspect of postponement.

❖ Write down a recent conflict with another person. Now distill a response as a Yes/And statement: Yes, I need to spend less, and we need to include priority items into our budget.

❖ Write down a recurring conflict in your sphere of influence. Now write out a hypothetical response. By not owning your dissenting opinion, you are able to deflect heat from the situation. At the same time, score! You're handling conflict.

❖ Describe a current conflict in your journal. Putting it down on paper lets you look at it from every angle. Now write down the impact of the conflict. What is going wrong because of the disagreement? Write down good questions to reflect upon when coming up with a good resolution.

❖ Write down something you routinely procrastinate doing. Now answer this question: What are the underlying issues? Don't write down you're lazy or you don't want to do it. Dig deeper and figure it out. Until you can isolate the underlying issues, you cannot change the dynamics of your behavior.

❖ Learn to reward yourself as you conquer the impossible. You always put off paying bills? Reward yourself with a treat each time you pay them immediately. You put off writing a report until the night before it's due? Reward yourself with some pizza as you tackle it immediately. See where this is going? You are establishing righteous habits, and you like it! For this to work, your response must be immediate. Be honest with yourself.

❖ Adopt the Nike trademark. Let Just Do It become you mantra. Everyone lives by a code of ethics and they are usually ensconced in cute phrases. Gibbs Rules. Princess Bride quotes. Add one to the mix. Write down your catch phrases, and add a new one to the list.

Step Three: Visualize

Can you see yourself as a strong person who handles conflict like a pro? Maybe you can name a role model you admire, someone who exudes confidence and diplomacy and always has the right words to say in any situation? Imagine yourself being that person. That's your goal.

Step 4: Set Goals

Where do you want to be in one month?

Name three tasks you can stop avoiding.

What is a reasonable time frame for becoming a diplomat?

Day Nine: Self-Forgiveness

Step One: Ponder

he next twenty-three days of exercises focus on feeding your soul. We've covered the giants standing in the way of productivity and measures for slaying them. Now we want to focus on ways to build you up, make you a more productive person.

The first thing to do is to forgive yourself for being in this predicament. We went through a lot of avoidance behaviors and negative traits in the first week, didn't we? Some of you are feeling pretty down with yourself right now. How did I let this get so out of hand? I didn't know there was so much wrong with me!

Well, there isn't. You're human. Give yourself a pass and let go of the past. Yes, you can. We're not dwelling on it. Period, end of paragraph.

If we don't talk about this for at least one day, you will be doomed to continue all those negative behaviors, looping all those bad habits. When you go back and complete more writing hacks on one of the prior topics, always end it with self-forgiveness. Don't let it mushroom into blame you either heap on yourself or someone else. Let go of the past.

I find that hard, and these are the tips that help me:

1. Recognize it is the past, and let it go. Easier said than done, right? Imagine a past incident that still bugs the heck out of you, and embody it. Shake hands with it and say, "Bye, bye!"

2. Recognize you are human, so stop expecting superhuman capabilities. Give yourself a little grace.

3. Identify the negative behavior at the basis of your procrastination. In popular terms, name it and claim it.

4. Formally forgive yourself. This works on mistakes large and small. I have to say, "I forgive you, Amy, for…" Try it.

5. Realize it didn't end the world. By putting things into perspective you put them into their proper place.

6. Start anew. That was the whole purpose of figuring out how your wires got crossed and setting goals for change.

7. Do something self-affirming. By now you can tell I'm big on rewards.

As you practice this concept of letting the past be past, it will get easier. The more often you go back and work on a negative quality, and each time work through self-forgiveness, it will become second nature.

Step Two: Write

❖ It's helpful to write out the steps listed above the first few times to let go of the past. Just Do It.

❖ If your procrastination has hurt someone in your life, deal with the guilt constructively. Write an apology and send it. Acknowledge your past and express your commitment to change. Do NOT do this through text or IM. Brief wording opens the door to all kinds of misunderstandings. Do NOT do this through email. It opens the door to a barrage of unhealthy back and forth exchanges, which only exacerbates the issue. Do NOT do this in person. Ambushing an apology when the other has no time for reflection never ends well. Writing down the precise words in your journal is a starting place. Transferring them into a note and dropping it in the mail allows time for a measured response. Now meet over coffee and let the past be past.

❖ Write down issues you still need to address. Being at peace with yourself is a prime way to become a stronger, more assertive you. These may include interpersonal conflicts, childhood issues or major offenses made by you or by others that have impacted you. Write down some dates for ticking these off your to do list. Because you tackled a biggie doesn't mean there aren't more issues living in the recesses of your mind.

❖ Borrow a scene from *Titanic*. Be the older Rose who climbs up on the railing and drops the Heart of the Ocean gemstone. Write down, "Oops!" Now list something you're letting go of. "I forgive myself for...."

Step Three: Visualize

Can you imagine a freer you? What will it feel like letting go of the burdens you've been carrying? How does a free person feel? Imagine yourself at peace, and let that image be the goal you're seeking.

Step 4: Set Goals

Where do you want to be in one month?

Name an affirmation you want to live by.

What is a reasonable time frame for being free of
the past?

Day Ten: Raise Your Self-Esteem

Step One: Ponder

Here's where you start rebuilding yourself -- not from the ground up, because basically you're okay. What you're looking for is a course correction, rewiring your brain in positive ways. One of the most important steps rests in realizing your full worth.

It's about having confidence in yourself, confidence in your abilities and confidence that you deserve the opportunities you enjoy. Let's look at the positive aspects. If you are strong and confident you:

- Can recognize the difference between confidence and arrogance
- You welcome feedback

- You are not afraid to state your opinion, even if it engenders conflict
- You set healthy boundaries
- You are not a slave to the monster of perfectionism
- You harbor no fear of failure

We talked about some of these giants causing procrastination, but now we want to hone in on ways to increase your core strength and build a healthy self-image.

Step Two: Write

❖ Face natural fears head on. A feeling of dread is normal when you get a call to report to the office, but remembering the good you've done should put it into perspective. Write down three things you've contributed or accomplished in the last month that make you smile.

❖ Reject personalizing comments of others. When someone criticizes an idea you've suggested, resist the temptation to think, "Well, he's never liked me anyway." A differing opinion is not evidence of any personal discrimination, even if there is a history of conflict. Write down a recent time when your opinion or suggestion was shot down, and then write about how you felt and the reasons why it may not have been personal.

❖ Rein in the tendency to respond negatively to criticism. You have a choice in how you respond. Write down a situation that made you feel insecure. Now, write down a response that acknowledges a difference of opinion without resentment, insecurity or passion. By measuring your words, you increase your own self-esteem.

❖ Reframe the meaning of a possible rebuff. You invited someone to join you and the response was, "No." Your first instinct might be to think either, "I'm unimportant" or "If I mattered, the answer would have been yes." An either/or construct sets yourself up for negativity. Instead, write down three reasons for the negative response.

❖ Develop healthy personal boundaries. You can end abuse from others. You can decide the level of friendship. You can determine how much influence others have over you. Write down where you want to draw the line in a relationship currently bothering you.

❖ Be kind to others. When you are self absorbed and always feeling inferior, you don't listen to others well. You fail to respond to needs and cues. Instead, spend time each day really listening to others, and write down some insights you gain. Your ability to empathize with others will increase your self-esteem.

Step Three: Visualize

Imagine what it would feel like to feel confident in your own skin. What would you wear? How would you walk? What kinds of things would you say? Being able to see yourself as a person worthy of respect is the beginning of expecting and receiving the respect of others.

Step 4: Set Goals

Where do you want to be in one month?

Name one daily action, every day, that you will implement to raise your self-esteem.

What is a reasonable time frame to grow comfortable in your own skin?

Day Eleven: Newton and Procrastination

Dana was an artist. She loved painting and sculpting and projects. Lots of projects. Dana married a physics teacher. She loved the way he honed all his focus on winning her affection. She admired his dedication to research. She appreciated his analytical mind and sense of humor until one month after they married.

All of a sudden, his maddening trait of wanting to accomplish projects around the house -- and wanting her help -- made her want to hide from him. His dedication to the task at hand drove her crazy when she had a spontaneous idea that far outweighed the pleasure of his drudgery. His analysis of the way she loaded the dishwasher, started the laundry or vacuumed the carpet incorrectly ignited several fights a day.

Fundamentally and diametrically opposite, Dana was a procrastinator and her practical husband was a "detail-oriented, opinionated, self-righteous zealot." Her words, not mine.

Clearly, their marriage suffered the effects of Newton's Third Law of Physics: for every action there is an equal and opposite reaction.

Step One: Ponder

When it comes to procrastination in any situation, be it a marriage or trying to work up the courage to attack the dishes in the sink, there exists a pair of opposing forces. The force impelling action is opposite to the force of feeling that says, "I can't face that right now." The paired interactions form a truth and a predictor of life. Opposites attract their other half of the Newton equation.

Let's look at this another way. While driving down the street a bug hits your windshield creating a nasty splotch right in your line of vision. The bug committed suicide by hitting your windshield and you murdered the bug with your car.

This is a clear case of Newton's Third Law of Motion. The bug hit your car and your car hit the bug. Which of the two forces is greater: the force on the bug flying or the force of the car? Most of us would claim our cars caused the interaction. Size matters. In truth, the forces were equal. If your car hits the bug, then the bug also hit your car.

Sounds inane, right? Let's apply this logic to the force field of your (or Dana's since it's really all about Dana, right?) procrastination. If your distaste for washing a mountain of dishes equals the first dish you wash, then all you need to wash is the first dish. According to Newton, it is that simple, and he was a genius.

Your reluctance to begin equals the first tiny step toward completion. Dreading writing a letter? Get out some paper and type a letterhead. That first tiny step propels you in predictable ways. According to Newton, a body at rest will remain at rest, and a body in motion (taking that first step) will remain in motion until forced to stop (like a bug splattering on the windshield).

James Clear wrote a whole book on the 2-Minute Rule. Do one small action to get the ball rolling, and you're much more inclined to finish it. In other words, your desire to complete the task follows that tiny first step as surely as day follows night. Looking at a mountain of dishes in your sink or any other equally distasteful task? Force yourself to work on it for two minutes. Take that one tiny action and see your procrastination in that task conquered.

Scientists claim that habits explain about 40% of what we do on any given day. Habits are a big deal, which is why Covey's Seven Habits of Highly Successful People has sold more than forty million copies in twenty-five different languages. A new habit, like breaking the cycle of procrastination, can be cultivated with five steps:

- Get a bird's eye view. Seeing things from a bigger perspective can help you know what you want to change. Decide what you want to change and why.
- Do that first small thing. Set an itty-bitty first-step goal.
- Give yourself grace. Missing a day isn't the same as quitting. When you

fall off the bandwagon, get up again. Quickly.

- Use old habits to build new habits. If you have a habit of sitting with a cup of coffee each morning, tie the new to the old. Sit with a cup of coffee each morning and *then* exercise.

- Create high stakes. No diet is more successful than a gal who is trying to get into a wedding gown. No exercise program works quite as well as a guy who wants to beef up for the team with a weigh-in one week away. Not getting married? Not trying out for the team? No problem. Invent a stake that *will* motivate your short term progress.

It has been said that it takes twenty-one days to create a new habit. Just twenty-one days, but no evidence proves it true. Decide to defy that logic.

Do one small thing and let it snowball into the life you want.

Step Two: Write

- ❖ Write down one thing you always put off until the last minute. Now write down one thing you could do to change the dynamic.

- ❖ If you're waiting for the pixie dust of inspiration, you're going to be waiting for a very long time. Instead, begin building one new habit. Write down what you want in your life.

- ❖ Take a cue from the stage. Building a new habit, like breaking the damaging cycle of procrastination, can begin with a cue of your own choosing. Set a reminder on your phone. The cue is enough to focus your attention on one small thing. Create a chart to monitor your progress.

❖ Reward your good behavior. Forget being an adult. Forget that doing a good job is its own reward. If you are trying to break the demon of procrastination in some area of your life, get out your favorite treat jar and start rewarding each and every miniscule accomplishment. Do one thing and get a reward. Of course this doesn't have to be candy. Start a Rewards Jar: write down little rewards on slips of paper and draw one each time. What would those rewards be?

Step Three: Visualize

What does the one thing you're going to do to align one piece of the procrastination wire puzzle your brain has made? Visualize putting one direct wire into your brain from a tiny task right to the spot where you want to park your new productivity.

Step 4: Set Goals

Where do you want to be in one month?

Name one tiny action you're willing to take to make your goal a reality.

What is a reasonable time frame to win this war on this one habit?

Day Twelve: Identifying Productivity Cycle/Patterns

Do the hardest jobs first. The easy jobs will take care of themselves."
Dale Carnegie

Step One: Ponder

The cycle of productivity is no mystery. Motivation leads to action. Action leads to productivity. Productivity leads to reinforcement of the pattern. And the beat goes on. It goes on if it has started hence this little age-old factor of procrastination.

The cycle begins with learning what motivates you. Perhaps you are reading this book because your teen procrastinates on his homework until the very last minute, ruining his chance for a scholarship and derailing the family with his last minute panic when everyone else is wanting to watch a movie. Perhaps you are reading this book because you procrastinate folding the laundry and everyone is tired of rummaging through the laundry basket to find a matching pair of clean socks. You bought this book for a reason. Let's look at establishing a pattern to reverse this procrastinating tendency.

Putting a program of productivity into place allows you to establish systems that keep you on track. For example, let's imagine you get swallowed up in Facebook when you should be getting something else done. Establishing a pattern of checking in right after each meal doesn't bar you from Facebook. It breaks the destructive cycle of spending too much time on social media. The result? You escape the hamster wheel of life. The pattern actually makes you more creative.

As you start to uncross those wires in your brain, you open up a lot of mental space for other things. Suddenly, starting that project isn't quite so overwhelming. You can increase the attraction even more by giving yourself a time slot for starting it. As it turns out, you are most creative when you are freed from the monster of undone work.

An added benefit of creating a cycle of productivity is the power of repetition in strengthening neural synapses. It's called the spacing effect. For example, students who procrastinate until they are forced to cram for a test actually retain less knowledge than those who study a small amount each day. Twenty minutes. That's the average retention of learning material with one exposure, like cramming for a test. The reinforcement of daily review is the action of learning. Our brains are able to retrieve that information when study is predicated on multiple associations or wires built into your brain.

Grouping your shots increases productivity. Associate a new task with one already being done, and suddenly you find yourself accomplishing double the amount of work in one setting. Multitasking doesn't work; instead, it spreads the effort being expended over a lot of tasks with none of them getting the full benefit of your focused attention. On the other hand, grouping tasks puts your focus on one task at a time, with a shorter completion time for getting all of them done.

Step Two: Write

❖ Daily cycles: Write down the items claiming your attention on a daily basis. Attach an item you typically procrastinate to one of them.

❖ Weekly cycles: What do you do once a week? Make a grocery list? Review sales? Write down one chore you detest and give it a weekly time slot.

❖ Monthly cycles: Wiping out the refrigerator shelves and giving your dog its flea medicine are two examples of monthly chores you could bundle for greater effectiveness. What is one area of procrastination you could relegate into a monthly task and stop fretting over?

❖ Quarterly cycles: Spring house cleaning is effective because of its cyclic nature. In the past, people deep cleaned when the smoke from the hearth fires for heating the house was over for the year. Like spring cleaning, there exist certain tasks you don't need to do very often, and some hold all the pleasure of quarterly taxes, which is none at all. Putting these age-old procrastination tempters into your calendar lets you focus on them only when they pop up on your schedule.

❖ You don't need to make this so complicated that it never happens. Work with your current schedule and be kind to yourself. You also don't need to reinvent the wheel. Start with a current habit. Put a new habit into place. Decide how often it needs to be done. Keep track of your progress. Write it into your planner or calendar. Now before saying you're done, reflect: Did you allow enough time? Is it too hard to accomplish in half an hour? Does it need to be broken down into smaller chunks? It's all part of the process.

Step Three: Visualize

What does the one thing you're going to do to break one piece of the procrastination wire puzzle your brain has made? Visualize putting one direct wire into your brain, from a tiny task right to the spot where you want to park your new productivity.

Step 4: Set Goals

Where do you want to be in one month?

Write down a new pattern of productivity.

What is a reasonable time frame to accomplish this pattern?

Day Thirteen: The Power of Written Goals

Step One: Ponder

There exists a universe between a wish and reality, and that universe is no wider than the stroke of a pen. A statement like, "I wish I was a better...." where you fill in the blank is not a goal at all. Yet most procrastinators think about their goals rather than writing them down in black and white. Written goals are the benchmark successful people point to when they describe their accomplishments.

It's true. Research has proven that 42% of study participants across all walks of life, irrespective of age or nationality, are more likely to accomplish their dreams (goals) by writing them down. Are you among the 58% who don't? That's why you're reading this book. You procrastinate. Your own body proves it true.

Within your brain live two different hemispheres divided by a structure known as the corpus callosum. Your right brain imagines the dream. Your left brain writes it down. If you are a dreamer who never writes down goals, the idea gets stuck in your right brain and never moves into action. By writing it down, you initiate a series of events that culminates in productivity. The impulse crosses the corpus callosum and takes up residence in the action-producing part of your brain.

Your right brain imagines it. Your left brain records it. The electrical impulses then elicit a charge to the fluid bathing your brain and traveling up and down your spinal cord. From there, muscles are activated and stuff happens. Cells in your muscles snap to attention and lo and behold, you find yourself a productive son-of-a-gun. Why? What did you do? You wrote it down.

Step Two: Write

❖ Begin an experiment. For the next seven days, begin the morning by writing down your goals. You can write goals for your health, relationships, your job, your time or your money. Don't limit yourself to past failures or the inner critic's voice judging what you've written. Revise the list each day to keep track of your accomplishments.

❖ Practice brainstorming your goals. Grab a pen and paper and write down all the ideas that pop into your head. You'll gradually see several that sound a lot alike. Gravitate toward one of them, and that will be your goal.

❖ Put a price tag on your goal. As early as 1955, researchers proved that goal-setting and money-making work hand-in-hand. In a landmark study, it was discovered at that time that only 3% of Harvard students wrote down goals. A review of accomplishments twenty years later proved those 3% made more money than the other 97% in combining all their assets. When you attach a dollar amount to your goal, you motivate yourself extrinsically, but growth occurs intrinsically, rewiring your brain.

❖ Write a goal and insert the word "achieve." It's magical. It makes a goal measurable and propels it from a theoretical exercise into a springboard for success.

❖ Write down a goal and then make a dream board. Adding pictures makes it real. Having a physical reminder is a way to grab your attention and focus your efforts on a daily basis.

Step Three: Visualize

Imagine your life if your goals were achieved. Where would you work? What kind of car would you drive? Where would you be taking your next vacation?

Step 4: Set Goals

Where do you want to be in one month?

Write down a benchmark for partially achieving this goal in one month.

What is a reasonable length of time for achieving this goal?

Day Fourteen: Dive-Bombing Distractions

Step One: Ponder

Many procrastinators are squirrels. The poor squirrel has gotten a bum rap. Put up a bird feeder and you'll see firsthand how tenacious the squirrels are in robbing it of food. Squirrels reproduce according to nut harvests, did you know that? Squirrels are master long-term planners, gathering and storing food each fall before winter sets in; don't pat yourself on the back quite yet if you are a squirrel.

Squirrels also represent roadkill when they get caught in the glare of headlights and can't decide which way to go. People earn the pejorative term of being a squirrel when they are easily distracted by two many impulses and possibilities. As a human being, you have higher powers. You can cognitively reason. You can hypothesize and devise many possible courses of action. You can choose the best option.

What you, in particular, seem unable to do is reduce distractions. Begin by taking charge of the things within your control. Disable notifications on your phone. Instead, check for important messages every half hour. You see, your distractions live below the level of your everyday life, below the consciousness of your activity. By syncing them you automatically cure some inclinations toward procrastination.

Step Two: Write

❖ Facing too many tasks paralyzes a squirrel with inaction. Write down all the many things occupying your brain. Next to each one, write a consequence of not accomplishing the task. From there you can put a star beside the one you'll do first and prioritize the rest.

❖ Learn how to delegate. Write down a list of things to accomplish and think of who could help with part of it. Letting it go is a huge part of getting it done.

❖ Write down the things that hold you back. These are your constraints. Compare your constraints to your list that overwhelms your productivity and cross out the items you can't accomplish. Do not move them to another day, which sets you up for failure.

❖ Up to 69% of us waste time every day during our most productive work hours. Those wasted moments are reflected in texting, social media, internet games and phone calls. Productivity takes a nosedive and we feel ambushed by distraction. Turn off the phone. Close windows to games. Write down how much time you want to award these distractions and write it into your day.

Step Three: Visualize

What would your life look like if you eliminated distractions from ruling your day? How would it feel to eliminate unwanted phone calls? Imagine a day in your life without distraction.

Step 4: Set Goals

Where do you want to be in one month?

Write down your three biggest time wasters and specific ways to reduce them.

What is a reasonable length of time for achieving this goal?

Day Fifteen: Schedule Shenanigans

Imagine sitting in a meeting. Everyone is seated in a circle with the facilitator occupying a seat opposite yours. He calls the meeting to order. You're nervous, it's your first time here. The facilitator rises to speak, but you hardly hear what he's saying. Then a woman sitting next to you speaks up.

"Hi, I'm Annie, and I'm a procrastinator." The room grows silent, and you suddenly realize you're in a circle of friends. Then you awaken, sweating. It was a dream after all. No one knows you are a closet procrastinator.

Step One: Ponder

One type of procrastination hasn't been discussed yet. Are you a closet procrastinator? Closet procrastinators fulfill certain kinds of deadlines with ease, often working ahead of time, but they postpone certain kinds of tasks every time they hit the cycle. Maybe you dread paying bills each month. Perhaps you procrastinate paying taxes until the Very. Last. Minute. If you keep this a deep, dark secret, you know something most people don't: You are an activity-dependent procrastinator. There is help for you, too.

One fatal flaw of activity-dependent procrastinators is that they tend to assign their most hated tasks to a future version of themselves, when they will presumably feel or be more ready. There is a total lack of emotional connection with this future self, in realizing that without taking action, nothing will be different. There exists an imaginary, heroic self who will emerge to save the day. Unfortunately, no cape or sword is relegated to the day when it arrives. If you are one of these people, scheduling may be your best friend.

Time block your commitments. The Pomodoro Technique is such a theory. Assign your task a time slot. Work in short, twenty-five minute bursts with scheduled five-minute breaks. There is even an app, Saent, designed for your laptop replete with a white button you can push to screen out all distractions. It features a progress bar to keep you on track. Sounds great, right? Before you rush to the app store, try using an egg timer first, to be sure this approach works for you.

Activity-dependent procrastinators may not need all that gadgetry. These tips may save you money and work better in the long run:

- Schedule periods to slack off. I know it sounds counter-productive, but giving yourself limited permission to procrastinate may jump start your productivity during self-assigned work periods.
- Experiment between longer blocks of assigned procrastination and shorter mini-breaks throughout the day. Which is more productive for you?
- Schedule easy tasks in the project first to build your confidence
- Schedule an unpleasant task or part of a project later. Even if you remain unmoved with the whole Nike Just Do It mentality, you can counter that

> resistance with the aid of your trusty planner.

This is taking time management to the extreme, and it will help limit tendencies toward procrastination.

Does scheduling work? A recent study looked at 250 adults who hate to exercise. They were broken into three groups, each assigned a different weekly task in addition to keeping track of their time working out. One read a novel. One read a tract on the benefit of exercise. The third set a schedule for when they would work out. Guess which group demonstrated the highest productivity, exercising more than the other two? Uh, huh. A whopping 91% of the third group actually exercised, compared to 35% in the first group and 38% of the second group.

Another study found that *when* you schedule your dreaded assigned task makes a big difference. Don't schedule it as the last task of the day or to be done late in the assigned work period. That is the same as procrastinating in the first place. It sounds like common sense, but having been an inveterate procrastinator myself, I'm aware of all the tricks. You're just deluding yourself.

A schedule creates a sense of value for you, and by extension, your time. Simply investing the time to write it down by extension adds value to the assigned task, and it tends to get accomplished. It was Peck who wrote, "Until you value yourself, you will not value your time. Until you value your time, you will not do anything with it."

Step Two: Write

❖ A planner is your new best friend to schedule those annoying tasks you don't feel like doing. Devise a coding system for triggering obedience. For example, write a task you've procrastinated with red ink, signaling the importance of starting.

❖ Find either a manual or electronic timer and use it for one day while keeping a log of your work habits. You will see patterns emerge, and can revise your process to increase your productivity.

❖ Create a system for evaluating each task when you complete it, with a score of one to five. If it was strictly pleasure, rank it a one. Strictly work? Give it a five. Assign numbers in-between for how important the task was for your success. The ranking system increases self-awareness and increases the pleasurable sensation of accomplishing something productive.

❖ Develop a system for prioritizing tasks. You can put stars beside them. Write them in different colors. Highlight them. The key is to make sure you know the most important thing to accomplish and get it done.

Step Three: Visualize

What would your ideal planner look like? Do you want a colorful cover or are you a down-to-earth minimalist? Do quotes quicken your mind? Do you like monthly, weekly and daily time separations? Do you want to buy a planner or make a planner? Visualize the perfect planning tool and then start making schedules.

Step 4: Set Goals

Where do you want to be in one month?

What is a reasonable length of time for finding the ideal planner?

How soon will you start using it?

Day Sixteen: Begin Seven Hours Earlier

Step One: Ponder

Productive people know how to get things done, and one successful practice of these annoying overachievers is that most of them begin the day seven hours ahead of you. That's right. They plan each day the night before. The process helps to reduce the fatigue of trying to decide what to do next which crushes your spirit in the morning; planning the night before organizes the day and results in an evening of celebration. You leave work behind because work is actually accomplished or planned.

Think of your tasks as assignments on Mission Impossible. Your mission, should you decide to accept it -- suddenly your mundane task assumes heroic proportions. Your missions become success strategies. Since by now you can crush scheduling, give each of these missions a time slot before you go to bed.

Organize your work before you begin. Write down what you will do, and be specific. Write down the tools you'll need. Where will you be doing this? Lay out your clothes. Organize your morning. These night-time rituals create a program for success. Why does it work?

- You'll sleep better knowing you have a plan.
- You will infuse your day with purpose.
- You will shift your mind into a proactive mode. Instead of reacting to crisis, you will be meeting the day head on and preventing crises from developing.

- Capitalize on that growing sense of empowerment as you become the hero you want to be.

Maximize this to your advantage by putting a Mark Twain truism into your life. He said, "Eat a live frog first thing in the morning and nothing worse will happen to you the rest of the day." Motivational gurus suggest eating the ugliest frog first. Plan on doing what you dread most as your first heroic mission of the day. The rest of the day and all your community will thank you. The truth behind this is simple: You will commit your future self to do things your present self procrastinates. The nastier the task, the more effective this strategy becomes.

For this to work, you must be honest. Don't overestimate your abilities or how quickly you can accomplish a heroic mission. You may need to pad a half hour into your schedule. If you find you routinely miss your mark, either break the task down into more manageable parts or add more time. And, hey, if you finish ahead of time, you already have a time slot for celebration.

An additional caveat: These important missions need to be accomplished by mid-morning at the latest. Every day poses its own challenges, initiates its own firestorms. Don't expect you can finish your night's plan in glorious afternoon sunlight. Be done by lunch.

Step Two: Write

❖ It doesn't matter when you're reading this: Write down an imaginary list that would have been important today. Practice the process.

❖ Remember this is a schedule, not a promise. Assess the effectiveness of your nightly ritual as you put the practice into play. Adjust, compromise. Devise ways to make it work. Mostly, write down things that went wrong and then cross them off. Forgive yourself when small failures threaten to derail the process.

❖ Write down a backup plan for when things go awry. Because the pandemonium theory of creation asserts they will. By having a plan, you avert disaster.

❖ Write down the distractions currently filling your morning. Drown the pings. Turn off the distractions. Avoid the pitfalls. If you can identify what interrupts your productivity, you can be the hero that vanquishes interruptions.

Step Three: Visualize

What does a night time ritual of planning look like? Do you do this before getting ready for bed or before turning out the light? Do you set out your clothes for morning? By visualizing how to do this, you make it 90% more likely you'll actually do it.

Step 4: Set Goals

Where do you want to be in one month?

What night will you start doing this? Tonight?

Day Seventeen: Sleep On It

Step One: Ponder

As it turns out, sleep is your friend.

The Bedtime Phenomenon is a newly coined term, but it's becoming more and more common. It happens when you mean to get to bed early, but end up binging on Netflix or staying up to read another chapter in a page-turner. Are pleasant distractions keeping you up at night? The results are disturbing.

Sleep procrastination is common for as many as one-third of all Americans. As it turns out, New York City isn't the only city that never sleeps. The internet brings together people from around the globe, and someone somewhere is up when they should be asleep. It's defined by the Center for

Disease Control and Prevention as being less than seven hours a night.

One of the less understood effects of sleep procrastination is the prolonged exposure to blue artificial light from the television, wreaking havoc on circadian rhythms and the production of melatonin. The self-perpetuating cycle becomes a routine and your health takes the hit.

Consider these alarming results of sleep deprivation:

- Experiencing one week of sleep deprivation affects your genes, the building blocks of cell replication.
- Sleep deprivation affects immunity, decreasing the white blood cells warring against infection.

- Sleep builds memory connections in the brain; a lack of sleep affects both short-term and long-term memory.

- Sleeping less than five hours a night increases the risk of hypertension, diabetes and heart disease.

- Chronic sleep deprivation can age your brain by three to five years and increase your risk of Alzheimer's Disease by 33%.

- One in twenty-five adults fall asleep at the wheel, endangering other lives besides their own.

- Sleep deprivation may cause a low libido.

- Chronic sleep deprivation commonly leads to depression. One-fifth of all insomniacs are diagnosed with depression.

- Sleep is responsible for growth and tissue repair. Losing sleep reverses the natural trend.

There is no question that sleep deprivation can be harmful, both as an incidental event or as a chronic malady. One problem is that sleep deprivation can itself lead to the inability to recognize its effects. Like the drinker who never recognize he's drunk, the inveterate sleep-deprived think they are managing just fine. They are superhuman. They require less sleep. Wrong. They are as human as the rest of us.

The sleep procrastinator will often procrastinate in other areas of life as well. Lower inhibitions, depression and heightened emotions all affect self-regulation when unpleasant tasks loom before them. Lack of sleep compounds the problem.

Does chronic procrastination of something so mundane as say, paying the bills, also affect your sleep? The answer is yes. Those who procrastinate simple things have a higher rate of insomnia, because subconscious worry robs them of their sleep. They suffer all the side effects of sleep deprivation, and something as simple as putting off cleaning the kitchen becomes a cause of something as serious of diabetes. That's not okay.

Step Two: Write

❖ Start a sleep journal and record when you go to bed at night, when you awaken, and when you finally rise. You can self-diagnose your problem by looking at the facts.

❖ The Sleep Foundation suggests ten minutes of cardio exercise before bedtime. Is this something you can do? Write down a list of activities you would do for seven consecutive nights, and track your sleep for those seven nights.

❖ Build good sleep habits. Add to the list as you research this topic and find life hacks that work for you. Keep track of how each tip works and employ the gold stars. Make a chart with hacks like:

1. Adjust the thermostat. The Sleep Foundation recommends 60-67 degrees.
2. Go to bed at the same time each night. It strengthens your circadian rhythms.
3. Develop a bedtime ritual.
4. Turn off electronics for a while before lights out.
5. Meditate before sleeping

6. Watch your reading habits. Don't read a page-turner.
7. Listen to soothing music.
8. Eat light snacks or drink non-stimulating beverages.
9. Spend time with your pet or family.
10. Don't waste non-sleeping time in bed. If you don't fall asleep promptly, get up, employ one of these hacks and try again.

❖ Make your bedroom the most peaceful room in the house. Write down things you like and dislike about your bedroom. Do you want a more comfortable mattress? Does clutter end up cluttering your mind? Does your closet need doors? Is your wall color too stimulating? Develop a short to-do list for making your bedroom a sleepy room.

Step Three: Visualize

See yourself getting ready for bed and falling asleep. Yup. It's that simple. If you can visualize the process for getting to sleep, you are that much closer to eliminating insomnia and rewarding yourself with some well deserved rest.

Step 4: Set Goals

Where do you want to be in one month?

What is your plan for the bedroom?

Day Eighteen: Take a Tip from Success Stories

Step One: Ponder

Self-proclaimed procrastinator Tim Urban is a popular guru on this topic because he built his success in life on overcoming the habit. His YouTube cartoons offer a creative and painful way to look at the dynamics involved in procrastination and how to get past them.

His format illustrates the progression of events from having a monkey standing by as you look at your schedule through the monkey taking the helm and forcing your cognitive reasoning aside until the monster of panic hits the scene. He puts a lot of faith into the Eisenhower model of drawing four quadrants and placing responsibilities into each of the four squares:

1. Important and Urgent
2. Important but NOT Urgent
3. Urgent but NOT important
4. NOT Important and NOT Urgent

He identifies procrastinators (and thus his former self) as living in quadrants three and four, while productive counterparts live in quadrants one and two. It's all downhill from there. Procrastinators get stuck in a loop between #1 and #3, but asserts that #2 in where productive people live.

In contrast, a procrastinator's model with four quadrants looks more like this:

1. Do It When It Goes From Urgent To Crazy-Important
2. Delegate It to Future You
3. Do It When #1 Is Urgent
4. Do It Now

The irony is that procrastinators never make it to #4. Procrastinators live in a world of wishes and dreams. They must create a world of tasks and obligations. Their ability to translate that great divide is the process of conquering procrastination.

Step Two: Write

❖ Finish this sentence: "Wouldn't it be wonderful if..." Identify a wish. Imagine an outcome. What you just wrote down is a wish. The difference between a dream and a goal is the difference between procrastination and productivity. Know your dreams.

❖ Write down an action plan. Your dream fulfillment requires moving from the mental to the physical. This doesn't have to be as detailed and specific as goal setting. It's a map from where you are to where you want to be.

❖ Write down what it's going to cost you to realize your dream. They come with price tags. Sleep? Time? Fellowship with a friend or loved one? Applied effort? Come to grips with reality if you want to make your dream your new reality.

❖ Write down the finish line for your dream. Be clear on what you want to accomplish. If you can dream it, you can create the finish line.

Step Three: Visualize

Dreaming big dreams is what makes you special. Don't stop! Visualize the transition of your dream to the goal that makes it come true. Can you visualize yourself completing the process for realizing the fulfillment of your hopes? It's part of the process.

Step 4: Set Goals

Where do you want to be in one month?

What are the goals you can implement to make your dream a reality?

What is a reasonable time frame to accomplish this?

Day Nineteen: Spank Yourself

Step One: Ponder

Self-discipline is the process of moving unpleasant extrinsic controls to internal, personally administered controls over behavior. A perfect storm of procrastination presents itself when an unpleasant chore comes face-to-face with a person who ranks high in being impulsive and lacking in self-discipline. Let's face it. You don't want to be on anyone's radar for a chewing out when a task goes unfinished. Whether it's a wife, a boss, a roommate or a team member, it's something you'd rather avoid.

How? By policing yourself. Research proves it, you'll be a happier person. Think of the most disciplined person you know. Do you think this skill came with birth? No. Somewhere along the path of life, it developed as a learned behavior. Obviously, that is easier if your were raised in a home where productivity and time commitments were emphasized. Not having that advantage doesn't have to define you.

- Self-discipline is a learned behavior and, no matter your age, it's not too late to start. Begin by removing temptations from your life. Eliminate time wasters, foods you know you can't resist. Don't let your environment, either at home or the office, sabotage you.
- Eat and sleep for maximum health.
- Begin before you think it feels right. You may not have a perfect situation, but self-discipline isn't about perfection. It's about learning to react purposefully to imperfect situations.

- Create breaks so you don't have to fudge to indulge. These are your lifelines along the path to change.
- Give yourself grace. You're going to slip once in a while. Forgive yourself and keep on going. These proven steps, consistently applied and worked upon, produce self-discipline.

The great thing about becoming a more disciplined you? You can apply this quality to other parts of your life. You will become more disciplined in your eating habits: yo-yo dieting will become a memory. You will become more disciplined in lifestyle demands and never waste money on late payments. You will become more disciplined in your work habits, and it won't go unnoticed. Self-discipline cuts across every part of your life and yields incredible dividends.

Step Two: Write

❖ Identify one, only one area of your life where you want to increase your self-discipline. Remember, this will affect all areas of your life, so don't go hog wild here. Write down one goal.

❖ Make a deal with yourself. You have to form a mental contract, a promise, if you will, and solemnly agree to honor the goal. Write it down in your planner. Put it on your mirror. Make yourself come face-to-face with the promise in many different ways.

❖ Write down your first step. Yes, that first step is often radical. Throwing away all the junk food in your cupboard hurts. It's a doozy, but it is imperative. If you throw temptation at yourself, you will fail. Write down this unimaginable first step.

❖ Write down a reward for yourself. Let it be glorious. A cruise? A trip to New York? A new outfit? Tickets to a game? The greater your reward, the more you'll strive to reach for it. Don't be a cheapskate here.

Step Three: Visualize

It doesn't matter how many times you have failed. This is the time you will succeed. Visualize the you who hits that coveted number on the scale. Visualize the you who gets that project done ahead of time. Visualize the you who breaks the vicious cycle of procrastination.

Step 4: Set Goals

Where do you want to be in one month?
What is your glorious first step?

What temptations are you removing from your life to get there?

When will you feel you've accomplished this goal?

Day Twenty: Don't be an Enabler

Step One: Ponder

If you are reading this because you live with a procrastinator, realize you may be part of the problem. Your significant other doesn't pay the bills on time? Doesn't do the dishes after each meal? You have a team member who doesn't do his/her fair share? And you help out? You may be enabling the very behavior that is making you crazy.

Stop saving the procrastinator!

- Realize you are not the procrastinator prosecutor. It's not your job to police or to save. Doing so only inserts a layer of resentment and complicates interpersonal relationships.

- Moreover, you stand between the failure and the success of another. When you prevent or remove evidence of procrastination, there remains no impetus for change.
- Protect yourself from the fallout. Make sure the consequences don't destroy your credit, affect your career, mess up your life. Seek the counsel of a life coach or manager if necessary.
- Have a Plan B to cope with a procrastinator's failure. You don't need to execute this plan, but you do need to have a fail-safe contingency.
- Realize you are an enabler.

What are the characteristics of an enabling personality? Do you avoid conflict to keep the peace? Do you minimize your procrastinator's tendencies? Do you tend to keep your emotions bottled up? Are you always hoping for a change?

Do you end up blaming and criticizing procrastination? Are you a life saver? These characteristics work against you when it comes to encouraging change. The more you enable a procrastinator to achieve success through your efforts, the longer you will swim in this choppy sea of conflict.

Step Two: Write

❖ Write down ways you have contributed to the problem. Until you identify your own counterproductive behaviors, you cannot set limits.

❖ Write down a fail safe measure for saving the world if your procrastinator does not come through. While you don't want to save a procrastinator from his/herself, you also don't want to throw out the baby with the wash water. Pick your battles, and don't make a life altering consequence the basis for success.

* Write down a script of how you'd approach a boss or life coach to get help for this situation. Knowing what to say, and rehearsing how you say it makes all the difference between being a snitch and being a responsible team member.

* Write down the behaviors you recognized in yourself that make you an enabler. What do you want to change? Write down how to get there.

Step Three: Visualize

What does a healthy you look like? Rather than continuing in codependent relationships, picture yourself being partnered in a relationship you deserve. Until you can visualize yourself and your behavior in more productive ways, you will find yourself reliving the same old destructive behaviors.

Step 4: Set Goals

Where do you want to be in one month?

What personality traits are you extinguishing?

How will you measure your success?

Day Twenty-One: Set Three Itty-Bitty Goals for Today

Step One: Ponder

Psychologists agree, here is your freebie: Dissecting an overwhelming "I can't" or "I won't" type of task into bite-sized chunks frees you to actually begin. This life hack takes all the information from Do One Thing on Day Eleven and Setting Goals from Day Fifteen and mashes them into a more comprehensive remedy for your delay tactics. This is perfect for procrastinators who look at the day and want to climb back into bed and sleep through it. The problem is that delaying the inevitable only adds to future pressure.

Setting three tiny goals makes any day strewn with too much debris more manageable. If you've been living with procrastination for a while, and if you've been trying to kick the habit, you probably recognize the fallacy of setting SMART goals: goals that are Specific, Measurable, Attainable, Relevant and Timely. Of course it sounds good. Some hot shot guru wrote it and it worked for him.

The problem is that you can procrastinate those incredibly SMART goals the same way you procrastinate everything else. As a matter of fact, you've probably procrastinated writing SMART goals in the first place. Why? Aaaah! Too much! If you're a procrastinator all that mumbo jumbo about measurements and specificity are sounding the death knell to getting it done. Like telling a depressed person to stop feeling sad, it doesn't work.

Instead, limit your expectations. Set three small goals. As you achieve them, your success will project you into a more productive rest of the day. To set small, itty-bitty goals, begin by asking yourself some questions. Basic questions. Forget something grandiose like, "What needs to get accomplished?" That's like saving the whales. Too big. Instead, ask yourself the kind of questions that jump-start productivity. "What interrupts my day?" "What is one thing I can do to make the situation better?" Setting a tiny goal that answers these questions pays off in larger dividends: You'll be more productive across the board.

Tim Ferriss in *The 4-Hour Work Week* advises, "Don't ever arrive at the office or in front of your computer without a clear list of priorities. I don't recommend using Outlook or computerized to-do lists because it is possible to add an infinite number of items. There should never be more than two mission-critical items to complete each day. Never." Did you catch that number? Two.

Alright, I recommend three, but are you getting the point?

Limiting your workload sharpens your focus. The first step in the process lies in limiting your start to the day. Three small goals. Begin. Get the day rolling. Dance in the aisles as you increase your productivity.

Step Two: Write

❖ Write down what your three small goals would have been today. What would have made the day different, more productive? Now, write down three small goals for tomorrow. Evaluate them each day, and learn how to be more effective.

❖ Practice distinguishing between a grandiose goal and a tiny goal. Write down a big ticket item, like saving the polar ice cap. Now write down one small goal. Recycle burnables.

❖ Write down what your three small goals would look like if you applied them to the grand scheme of the universe. Do you see how they fit in? Good.

Step Three: Visualize

How do you think you will feel if you can reduce the load of having way too much off your shoulders? Visualize your face with less worry, your shoulders less hunched, your eyes without a glazed expression. Learn to identify the difference between feeling stressed and feeling relaxed despite your workload. That's the place where you want to live.

Step 4: Set Goals

Where do you want to be in one month?

How many days do you plan on practicing this hack?

Day Twenty-Two: Make It a Priority

Step One: Ponder

We do what we have to do, isn't that right? A crying baby demands attention. A ringing phone has to be answered. A whistling kettle? *Make the noise stop!* The problem with a task we procrastinate is that it isn't urgent. Or is it? Many procrastinators never recognize that a) they are procrastinators and b) that they're addicted to the behavior.

Those who do exhibit self awareness and have tried to stop but can't, find it's like trying to force like poles of a magnet together. Telling a procrastinator to "Just do it" is like telling a depressed person to "Just cheer up." Fat chance.

Instead, if you're a procrastinator, work on your sense of urgency.

When you don't set your priorities, you end up following the path of least resistance. Thoreau penned, "The path of least resistance leads to crooked rivers and crooked men." It also leads to fewer new opportunities and less income. Growth is always on the edge of the vine. It involves risk: I urge you to be a daredevil. Take a lesson from this country love song:

"I hope you never fear those mountains in the distance. Never settle for the path of least resistance. Livin' might mean takin' chances, but they're worth takin'. Lovin' might be a mistake but it's worth makin'."

Lee Ann Womack

Urgency serves as a precursor to action. By injecting a deadline, realizing the importance of a task or rehearsing the consequence of failure, you instill a sense of urgency and the task becomes a priority. It keeps you from wasting time on the unimportant, and you will find yourself more willing to do the one thing that matters.

Step Two: Write

❖ Write down the single most important thing in your life. Most of your tasks exert little impact on this priority, but some will impact you indirectly. Figure that out.

❖ Write down five things currently stressing you out. Write a priority that eliminates those stressors.

❖ Remember the things you can control, most notably your reaction to life events. Write down a priority that enables you to react in a way that increases your self-respect.

❖ Make gratitude a priority. Once a week, make it a practice to recognize the people who help you succeed in life. Write thank you notes or texts or emails.

Step Three: Visualize

Visualize a day in which you make your life represent your priority. What things will you do? What things get eliminated?

Step 4: Set Goals

Where do you want to be in one month?

How many days in a row do you plan on setting one priority?

Day Twenty-three: The Power of DNA

Step One: Ponder

There exists evidence that procrastination may relate to your genetic makeup. A study of twins over time indicated that since it occurs in both individuals, inherited tendencies may be indicated. Each exhibited the same dopamine levels, regulating their self-control and tendencies toward being impulsive. Certainly each twin shared life experiences, but their reactions were not always the same, indicating an inherited trait. Before you give yourself a pass on this, realize each person is born with positive and negative traits.

Excusing a negative trait because it may have an inborn tendency is like saying, "I can't stop at a traffic signal because I was born this way, Officer." It doesn't take you very far from the central point. You are expected to rise above your inborn tendencies, not use them as an excuse for poor performance.

This is an explanation and a warning, not a way out. Yes, procrastination may run in your genes. It is linked to families and no data distinguishes whether it is a learned behavior or an inborn trait. But before you rush to excuse yourself, realize that you may be the next in a self-perpetuating destructive cycle. You are modeling this behavior to younger eyes and they are patterning their lives after your actions.

It's important to realize that you are creating another generation of procrastinators if you fail to rein in your own bad habits.

If you live with a procrastinator, stop enabling those tendencies as you complain about the relationship. If you've been picking up the slack, assume responsibility for your part in the problem.

Step Two: Write

❖ Write about a parent or grandparent from whom you learned or inherited this tendency of procrastination. How was it destructive in the past? By learning from the mistakes of the past, you can change your present.

Step Three: Visualize

Visualize the words you'd say to forgive the parent from whom you learned procrastination. And visualize the words you say to the child you're influencing. Realizing how much you don't want that conversation helps prevent it.

Step 4: Set Goals

Where do you want to be in one month?

List three goals in creating a healthier relationship.

Day Twenty-four: List It

Step One: Ponder

Maybe you learned about the power of lists when you were young and were asked to write out a Christmas wish list. Sometimes that didn't turn out so well, but you weren't in charge of wish fulfillment back then. Now you are. Making a list makes a goal that much easier to hit.

I'm a list-maker from way back. I make lists and then make lists of my lists to be sure I don't lose them. There's power in making a list. For one thing, I remember things better. If I forget my list, I can remember half of it from conjuring up a memory of what it looked like on the page. As I make a list, I add sublists of things to do, so the objective takes place. Planning an event. Teaching a class. Making a quilt. All of my to-do's begin then come into existence because they had a place on a list.

One study confirmed that by writing a list of things to do, the participants had a 33% greater tendency of accomplishing the goal. See what's happening here? I alluded to it above. Your list becomes a subset of actions for accomplishing your goals. Whisper with me: "That's very powerful."

How do you get started? Begin by asking yourself these questions:

- How much money do I want to make next year?
- What luxury would I like to purchase?
- Where do I want to live?
- Where would I travel if money was no object?

As you answer those questions, goals begin to form in the back of your mind. Now, choose one item from this list and make a new list of what it would take to achieve it. You are well on your way to becoming a listaholic. Check something off on that list and you'll be hooked for life.

Experiment with different platforms. If you're a gadget geek, use a tablet or smartphone app. I like the organic process of putting a pen to paper. Sometimes I put my lists into the calendar on an hourly reminder of appointments, but more often I attach them to client charts. Try out different methods and choose the platform that works best for you.

Don't overwhelm yourself with too many actionable items on your list. If you have more than eight, you need sublists. Assign lists to subsequent days. You may also color code your lists. If number one has a subset of six items, make both lists on blue paper. Devise a system that works for you. It is also helpful to establish a master list, and from it devise a daily list.

One proven technique is the Ivy Lee method. Take fifteen minutes at the end of your workday and list a few tasks, not more than five or six. Prioritize them and list them in order. In the morning begin on number one. Do not move on until it is accomplished. Then focus on number two. If any remain, revolve them into tomorrow's list. If this sounds too structured for you since, after all, you've been a procrastinator for quite some time, it's okay to fly by the seat of your pants -- with a list.

Step Two: Write

- ❖ Do you write grocery lists or to do lists? Write one now.

❖ Extend that exercise by writing a list of all the vacation spots you'd like to visit. Imagine the world. Money is no object. Neither is time. You have unlimited vacation. Make the list.

❖ Make a list of supplies you need to do this. I like a pretty cup for my pens. I need lots of different colors and one or two need to be cute. I also need all kinds of paper. Yes, I make lists on napkins in restaurants when I'm in a panic. I do my best work with lovely paper and a hot pink pen. What about you?

❖ Go back to one of our sessions on setting goals. Revisit a goal and make a list of steps to make it happen.

❖ Now apply this to your nemesis in the world of procrastination. Write down the one thing you procrastinate the most. List steps to getting it done.

Step Three: Visualize

Visualize yourself making a list. What are you drinking? What time of day is it? Where are you? All of this makes a difference in seeing yourself as a list maker.

Step 4: Set Goals

Where do you want to be in one month?

What kinds of lists do you want to make?

Day Twenty-five: Build On Success

Step One: Ponder

Do you remember building towers as a child? A tower is built block by block, stacking one block on top of another. Success in life happens that way, too. One step leads to a promotion to a connection to the next job. Paying the bills leads to satisfaction that leads to a good night's sleep. No matter what you routinely procrastinate and what you want to accomplish, you have to build your success story.

A number of strategies are involved. Coined by S.J. Scott, Habit Stacking describes the concept of adding five minute tasks on top of each other to build a tower of efficiency and routines of success. Researchers hypothesize that habits account for forty percent of our behaviors. That's a lot of routine, people. We talk about building habits, building firm foundations, climbing the ladder of success. Do you ever wonder why so many analogies revolve around the principles of construction?

It's because you weren't built in a day. Your procrastination became habit and your wires got crossed somewhere in the building process. It takes some demolition of old ways to build new ways into your subconscious. You do that by laying new neural pathways, building on success, from one success to the next.

Begin with the idea of the procrastination habit you want to demolish. You know why it's damaging your life.

Arm yourself with the right tools. Forget willpower. It's a muscle subject to fatigue and it makes your head hurt. The right tools are easier to use. Write down what you're going to do. Assign a time. Move your hand. What did you use? Your hands. That's right. You have everything you need to build a successful habit.

Increase your new habit in small ways. Don't overdo it. Imagine every success in doing your new habit as a one percent increment of improvement. Keep doing it. Add up your progress. Before long, you'll see measurable improvement.

Build on that success.

Step Two: Write

❖ Write about a success in your life that leap-frogged you to a second success.

❖ What does success look like to you? Is it money? Is it a certain house or neighborhood? Is it what you drive? Define success.

Step Three: Visualize

Visualize yourself with the success you want to experience. Imagine yourself right down to what you're wearing and what you're doing. If you're not smiling, you're not taking this seriously.

Step 4: Set Goals

Where do you want to be in one month?

Name three things that will start the process of building your success.

Where do you want to be in one year?

Day Twenty-six: Wake Up Early

Step One: Ponder

Does the early bird really get the worm? Actually, yes. A heavy rain brings juicy worms to the surface and they don't remain there long. Hungry birds gobble them up, forcing latecomers to dig for their breakfasts.

Success stories are built in those early morning hours. Apple CEO Tim Cook sets his alarm for 3:45 am. Sound drastic? Not once it becomes a habit. Life's success stories are often early risers. Elon Musk, Bill Gates, Larry Ellison and Arnold Schwarzenegger all wake up early. Greats like Daniel Webster, Benjamin Franklin, Theodore Roosevelt and Ernest Hemingway, too. They established routines to structure their days.

Research proves there is a cause and an effect between being an early riser and achieving goals.

Research further confirms that sleeping late correlates with avoidance procrastination. Add to this finding the subjective well-being research subjects described in conjunction with rising early, and you begin to see a beneficial pattern emerging. You're a night owl, you say? I get it.

Here are some tips to make the transition easier:

- Arrange your room, if possible, to allow natural light to enter.
- Have an alarm clock at the ready, but not too close. That snooze button needs no help.
- Eat a hearty breakfast.
- Devise a plan for using the extra hours you're up to productively make it all worthwhile.

- Every so often, reward yourself by attending a breakfast club or early social event.
- Make sure your alarm clock is annoying enough to make you get up to turn it off.
- Create morning rituals.
- Devise a slow transition into this new lifestyle. Ease into it.
- Don't linger in the bedroom. That's like putting the fox in charge of the hen house.

Step Two: Write

- List three things you'd accomplish if you got up an hour earlier each day. Make sure these are things you'd really like to do.

❖ Write down one tip from the above list you want to try.

❖ Write a thank you note to yourself, and tuck it under your pillow. Use it to remind yourself why you're getting up early.

❖ Have you ever watched the sun rise? Get up early tomorrow and write about the experience.

Step Three: Visualize

Imagine yourself up in time to watch the sun rise. Imagine your favorite brew in your favorite cup. What do you think you're feeling? (Don't say tired.)

Step 4: Set Goals

Where do you want to be in one month?

Set a goal for the number of days each week you want to rise early.

Day Twenty-seven: The Grand Canyon View

The Stonecutters Tale

One day, a traveler came across three stonecutters working in a quarry, each busy cutting a block of stone. Interested, the traveler asked the first stonecutter what he was doing. "I am cutting a stone!" Still no clearer to an understanding, the traveler turned to the second stonecutter and asked the same question. "I am cutting this block of stone into a perfect square with uniform dimensions, so it will fit into an exact space on the wall," the second replied. A bit closer to understanding the stonecutters' goal but still unclear, the traveler turned to the third. He appeared the happiest of the three. When the traveler asked what he was doing, the third stonemason replied, "I am building a cathedral."

Step One: Ponder

A stunning vista causes us to drink in all the scenery at once. We want to look at the big picture. Evolutionary tendencies work against procrastinators here. We come wired with a focus on the present: the next meal, the next ten minutes, the next crisis. Psychologists have a term for it: temporal discounting.

Like the first two stonecutters, procrastinators put their attention on the present -- going here or doing that, rather than perceiving the ultimate goal. Learning to distill the overall objective, figuring out what matters most versus what details are insignificant, is a skill that anyone can learn.

Your tendency to hone in on immediate details or tasks needs to be tempered with your view of the overall objective. For example, you need to balance the checkbook and pay bills. You begin, but soon you're obsessing over an increase in your trash bill and that prompts you to check the last four months of trash bills, and that prompts you to look at sites to compare rates of competing companies, and whoa! You are no longer balancing the checkbook and paying bills. Begin any task with a clear understanding of your priority and keep a to do list at your elbow. Write down your top priority if it isn't specified on your list. Set a timer to ding every ten or fifteen minutes as a reminder to realign your activity with the main priority. If you deem a further investigation of trash bills is warranted, add it on the to do list at you side. These simple actions allow you to focus on the task at hand while keeping the big picture in mind.

It's a matter of vision. You want a panoramic vision of your life and where you're headed, rather than having tunnel vision over obscure details. Of course you need to focus on the right vista with your own Grand Canyon directly in front of you. Ask yourself a few grounding questions: What does this mean for your grade or your career or your life? Are you on your way to a desired end or are you floating through life and discontent? You want to see yourself as the third stonecutter doing a specific task for a greater good. That new perspective can propel you into the right direction.

Step Two: Write

❖ Write down the task you procrastinated on most. What is the bigger purpose involved in its completion? Seeing the value helps you attend to the details.

❖ What is the value of the bigger picture in your life? Doing your job and paying the bills isn't much of a life. Write down a bigger goal that gives meaning to your life, and if you can't come up with one, list some changes you'd like to make.

Step Three: Visualize

Visualize standing at the edge of a grand vista. That vista is your future. What does it look like? What do you want it to look like?

Step 4: Set Goals

Where do you want to be in one month?

Where do you want to be in one year?

What do you want your life to look like in three years?

Day Twenty-eight: Stop Worrying About What Others Think

Step One: Ponder

Ask a beauty queen how she looks. Her first instinct may be to point out her crooked nose. Every person on the planet grows up self-conscious. The plague isn't inborn, it is learned. Toddlers show their atrocious artwork with the greatest of pride. Kindergarteners believe a job well done is coloring in, on and outside the lines. Little ones are comfortable in their own skin and confidence exudes from them like a mantle worn with pride.

Somewhere along the way that changes. Being told to color *inside* the lines for the umpteenth time clicks, and tiny extensions beyond the black line become reason for embarrassment. The trend continues, and some of us grow shy or insecure being noticed by others. It culminates in a population of neurotic adults who worry incessantly about what others may be thinking about them.

As an adult, that tendency surfaces when asked to speak in front of a group or when all eyes turn toward you in a social setting. The resulting anxiety erodes confidence in yourself. You must first learn to keep a different perspective uppermost in your mind, to relieve the stress once it settles upon you. Not keeping a handle on it leads you to procrastinate certain tasks because you worry about how others will judge your performance.

Some tips to give you a dose of reality:

- People are more concerned with themselves than they are with you.

- You are being sabotaged by your own mind. Stop agreeing with negative thoughts.

- Work on building your self-esteem.

- Realize you are procrastinating to protect yourself from projected negative outcomes no one has made.

- Learn to work in the flow of things, losing yourself in the task. This reduces your awareness of yourself, and thus reduces your anxiety over perceptions.

- Adjust your internal standards. One reason why you are self-conscious is because you think you should perform better and, by extension, others must think so as well.

- Give grace liberally. The less you judge the performance of others, the easier it is to cut yourself slack.

Studies indicate that procrastinators are often dependent on others. Because you lack a strong sense of self, you rely on the perceptions of others to assess your own self-worth. You rely on others to suggest how you look, to rate your performance, to decide if you measure up. That tendency causes you to procrastinate because they haven't given you the go-ahead on a given project, so how can you possibly proceed?

Other research suggests that procrastinators are hard on themselves. You are lenient with a coworker about their performance on a project, but expect yourself to get it done on time and with great precision. Your exaggerated view of what you *should* be able to do indicates an elevated opinion of your abilities. Fear you can't measure up to the ideal in your own head causes you to procrastinate.

The ultimate result is that no one can judge your performance because you didn't have enough time, you didn't have enough resources, it isn't indicative of your capabilities. All of this stems from worry over how others perceive you. Let's work on that.

Step Two: Write

❖ Write down a realistic assessment of yourself. Be fair and non-judgmental. Compare that to what you are experiencing when you procrastinate a common task.

❖ Think about a subtle form of judging you perform on others. List people in your sphere of influence. What overarching trait would you give each one? Too opinionated? A busybody? Too direct? Contrast those judgments with a more rounded assessment of each person's strengths. Your judgement of others has been affecting how you think they must be judging you.

❖ Write down a dozen affirmations about your own abilities and self-worth. Put them in a little jar and when you catch yourself thinking negative thoughts, pull one out and believe the positive message you're reading.

Step Three: Visualize

Visualize yourself with no anxiety standing in front of a group of people. Rather than focusing on what you're wearing or how you are presenting yourself, notice how you feel. That confidence is your goal as the norm in your life.

Step 4: Set Goals

Where do you want to be in one month?

Where do you want to be in one year?

What do you want your life to look like in three years?

Day Twenty-nine: Derail the Tendency to Give Up

Step One: Ponder

Many a procrastinator begins with good intentions, but puts a task aside rather than completing it. You have a dozen reasons, don't you? Let's look at a few.

Sometimes the task threatens to overwhelm you. It's natural for a new task to be confusing. A term paper looks like a tangle of unrelated facts until there is an outline. The solution? Build a time slot for confusion into your assignment. By giving yourself time to figure out the steps or create an outline, you limit the tendency to get caught like a deer in the headlights when a task gets overwhelming.

Sometimes other responsibilities demand your attention. These pesky items draw you down a rabbit hole that lead you away from the task at hand. The key is to write a NOT To Do List at the outset. List all your distractions and add to it if another threatens to drag you off course.

Commit to your task publicly. There's nothing like posting that you're writing your term paper on Facebook to force yourself to come through. No one wants to be seen as a quitter by a few hundred online friends. That public announcement of your intention will help you stay on course.

Focus on the takeaway. In a California study, children were given the choice of eating one marshmallow now as opposed to waiting fifteen minutes and eating two. Those able to delay instant gratification benefited from the wait. Long-term analysis of the test subjects revealed that thirty percent of the children able to wait experienced later success in life. When you focus on the bigger reward, the result gives you some added oompf when quitting tickles your brain. Learn to be kind to your future self. Quitting a task sets you up for repeated failures, and your future self will need to adapt to that reality. Give your future self a name. Think of his or her best interests. Give your future self a better chance in life by not quitting now.

Step Two: Write

- ❖ Self-forgiveness is a crucial part of keeping your goal on target when you're faced with change. Write down a simple note of forgiveness and print it out. Tuck it into your planner for those days when you feel like throwing in the towel. Forgive yourself and carry on.

❖ Procrastination has become a life addiction for you. Realize the strategies that you are employing may be lifelong actions. Write down two motivations for continuing your strategies when you don't feel like it's going well.

Step Three: Visualize

Visualize a time when you experienced success. What did it feel like? Visualize what your life will look like when you no longer procrastinate. Imagine wearing a medal. Be a superhero -- especially to yourself.

Step 4: Set Goals

Where do you want to be in one month?

Do you have a date for no longer being a procrastinator?

Day Thirty: Solving for the Situation

Step One: Ponder

Chronic procrastination occurs when certain tasks always get overlooked and then are slotted for the panic button. A certain task at a critical juncture becomes too difficult, too many variables affect the outcome, too many conflicting choices are presented. You have to solve what to do in that situation, and your natural solution is avoidance. You procrastinate.

Overcoming procrastination involves developing one of the traits employers value most: problem solving skills.

Step Two: Write

❖ Practice turning a negative situation into a positive one. Write down a positive description of a task you've been avoiding. Make sure it has a positive spin. Don't you feel a more positive attitude toward it now?

❖ Write down a task you typically procrastinate. Now look at it from several different perspectives. How would an employer see it? What about a professor? What about a companion or friend? What about a family member? Seeing it from multiple perspectives helps prevent analysis paralysis from setting in. With a clearer view of the problem, you are less likely to procrastinate.

❖ List the steps to preventing the problem or situation. Your procrastination routinely puts you into panic mode before taking action. Find the key to doing it before it becomes a "situation."

❖ Apply the problem solving process to several issues. Do you see a pattern? Write down a format you can use the next time you think about procrastinating because of the situation.

Step 3: Visualize

Imagine what it must feel like to be a problem solver. Sense how others view this new capability, how it may be rewarded in the workplace, how it is appreciated in your home life.

Step 4: Set Goals

Where do you want to be in one month?

Do you have an end date on this?

Day Thirty-one: Thirty One Simple Life Hacks

1. Finish what you start. Some chronic procrastinators begin but have trouble finishing projects.

2. Stand up. Move. Get your blood pumping. Refocus.

3. Get an accountability partner. You may need to have your feet held to the fire. That's okay.

4. Post It Note Reminders. Millenials use Iphones and high tech gadgetry. Utilize some form of reminder for what you need to do.

5. Let your inner artist shine. Be creative in any medium you enjoy and it will boost your productivity in arenas where projects earn your bread and butter.

6. Set the alarm -- get up earlier.

7. Get all the sleep you can. Go to bed at a reasonable -- and consistent -- hour.

8. Tidy in 15 minutes. Assign short time slots for clearing your desk and throwing away accumulate, useless paper.

9. Slash your entertainment budget. Get rid of expensive cable plans and spend less time staring at the box.

10. Discipline for Positivity. Banish negative thoughts and replace each occurrence with a positive thought.

11. Do one thing.

12. Create a time block

13. Make a list. Scratching things off is orgasmic.

14. Check emails in the last hour at the office. It allows you to avoid the sinkhole of unproductive hours being sunk into correspondence and enables you to end your day with a summary of progress.

15. Disengage from social networks -- at least during work hours.

16. Automate processes not requiring your personal attention.

17. Keep track of your time.

18. Assess how you spent the time you tracked.

19. Name your enemy. By figuring out what you procrastinate, you can begin to defeat the inclination.

20. Don your headphones. A playlist of music you love may be exactly the right antidote for banishing distractions.

21. Let good enough be good enough. Create parameters for your project. When you've met them, STOP. It

doesn't have to be perfect. It has to be done.

22. Set goals. Every day.

23. Keep track of your blocks of time. Avoid time traps by keeping an eye on the clock.

24. Reward your accomplishments.

25. Forgive yourself when you slip. Clark Kent had kryptonite. You are not Clark Kent.

26. Say, "No," to some projects. If you overdo it, your project will fail.

27. Institute "Quiet Time." Everyone needs moments of silence, and you shouldn't have to escape to the

bathroom to find it. Create your own oasis in the middle of your work day.

28. Write down your bottom line. Be clear with yourself on your own expectations. Give yourself an ultimatum.

29. Create measures of perseverance. How many minutes did you focus on a particular task? Write it down in your calendar, and track your own performance.

30. Put the Pareto Principle to work for you. This truism establishes the 80/20 ratio, and you can make it work for you. Do 80% of the work in 20% of the time.

31. Utilize if/then statements: if I do this work, then I will succeed; if I fail to get this done, then I won't succeed. You'll find the results highly motivational.

The idea behind 31 Life Hacks is simple. You've read the research. You've worked through thirty-one days of interactive projects. Employ these hacks to streamline your productivity. This book is designed for consistent and repetitive practice on the facets of procrastination affecting you the most, which is why you were given multiple writing assignments in each of the exercises. Repeat the whole process. Go back to face your nemesis. Make productivity your goal and you will not be disappointed. I'm honored by your invitation to join you in the process.

Part III: FAQ

- **Is procrastination a mental illness?**
It is not listed in the American Psychiatric Association's Diagnostic and Statistical Manual of Mental Disorders, but when it affects the quality of life, it assumes gigantic proportions. As the incidents continue to rise, and the effects on society increase, that delineation may change.

- **Does the Digital Age make procrastinating easier?** Of course. Technology is not your friend, especially when it claims you attention at all hours of the day and night. More insidious than its invasion into all parts of our lives is its tendency to enhance habits of instant self-gratification. When you add its propensity to shorten attention spans with small bytes of information, you can see why it has such a pernicious affect in our lives. Life promises to only get more complex, however, so it's time to figure out how to live with that complexity than fight against it.

- **Why is procrastination so hard to change?** "When we procrastinate, our present self benefits from mood repair, while our future self stands to bear the cost of the delay. The thing is, we don't worry much about our future self; we actually think about our future self more like a stranger."

Pychyl, Timothy A. March 2018. Psychology Today. https://www.psychologytoday.com/us/blog/dont-delay/201803/how-negative-thoughts-relate-procrastination

- **Doesn't everyone procrastinate? Isn't it normal?** No, it's not. Procrastination is a learned trait, not an inherent quality in anyone's psyche. It develops early in life and is reinforced often by autocratic parents who never let a child internalize his own self-discipline. Such a child turns to friends for support, who have no interest in shaping or molding their friend for success. The result is self-sabotaging behavior throughout life, unless the individual chooses to grab himself by the lapels and force himself to change but he may put that off, too. Hence, the seriousness of the problem.

- **Is procrastination the same as being lazy?** We're looking at two different things here. A procrastinator chooses to wait, while the lazy person (apathetic, inactive, unwilling to act) refuses to choose an action. The results may be the same, but the motivation is derived from two very different personality traits. Name it and claim it in order to change it.

- **Can depression be linked to procrastination in any way?** These self-destructing twins often co-exist, and the real question is whether depression results in procrastination, or does procrastination cause depression? A study in Toronto cited the unsurprising relationship between these two dark twins: the more depressed we are, the more we procrastinate, and vice versa. There was, however, one surprising outcome: when self-regulating skills were controlled, the relationship between the two disappeared. This offers huge implications for those who want to break the destructive cycle. *It can be done.*

Pychyl, Timothy A. June, 2013.
Psychology Today.
https://www.psychologytoday.com/us/blog/dont-delay/201306/depression-and-procrastination

- **How do I figure out what types of strategies/techniques will help me the most?**

1. Unfortunately, there is no crystal ball with your name on it. You'll need to experiment and find what works for you. You don't expect your friend's diet and quick weight loss to be something that works for you and why would you? We are all different. Different hormones, neurotransmitters and life experiences dictate what will work for

you. Try new things. Be a goal digger. Look for the very best strategies for your own life.

2. As you go through the 31 life hacks, begin each day with a quick review of the day before. Grade each activity for its personal effectiveness in your life. If that hack worked for you, give it a five star review because that's a coping mechanism you can revisit time and again.

- **How do I make sure I don't lose motivation in the future?** Trust me, you will. Like any addiction, learning to live without procrastination is a concept you will need to address throughout your life.

- **When do I need professional help?** For some people,

procrastination is more than a bad habit. It's part of the ADHD or OCD personality. Seek a psychologist and/or a healthcare professional for therapy.

Part IV: Overview

If you are a procrastinator, you've probably been employing various coping techniques to try and get by, and they aren't healthy.

- Denial: pretending you're not procrastinator; you're an incredibly busy person.
- Justification: pretending you work better under pressure.
- Avoidance: pretending other tasks are more important.
- Distancing: pretending you don't care about the outcome.
- Trivializing: pretending it's not an important thing to learn or do.

- Comparing: pretending your procrastination isn't as big a deal as someone else's failure.
- Valuing: pretending your ability to work under pressure is heroic.
- Laughing: pretending your procrastination is funny.
- Distracting: pretending other things demand your attention.
- Deflecting: pretending everyone else is to blame for your failures.

All these behaviors involve pretending you don't have a problem. If you want to conquer the procrastination plaguing your life, you must accept that you have a problem and take action to counter the tendency.

By now you realize procrastination is an acquired, addictive behavior. As characterized by William Gibson, addictions start out like magical pets doing extraordinary tricks and are fun. Gradually, addictions begin to make decisions for you. Eventually, your addiction started making your most crucial life decisions, and let's face it, addictions are less intelligent than goldfish.

The discussion and life hacks presented in this book changed that alchemy. In the first four chapters you learned the basis of your addiction, recognizing latent tendencies in your own personality. With opportunity for reflection and journaling, you took action to incorporate needed changes in your behavior, changing your mindset. The 31 life hacks took you from using lame coping mechanisms to the empowering ability of facing life head-on, tackling those things you procrastinated in the past. You discovered the real you in the many descriptions and exercises and proactively rewired your brain to eliminate old habits and build new ones. Give yourself a pat on the back! You have achieved what so many of your friends and colleagues have not: self-control.

Final Words

Thank you for inviting me into your home, for visiting with me while curled up with a cup of tea. I've loved imagining you with your journal and a favorite pen at the ready as I've invented these exercises and plotted your progress. Your usual place for study, reflection and journaling must become a place of sanctuary for you, as you continue to implement the changes you're wiring into your brain.

We've enjoyed a fruitful journey together, haven't we? The rewiring of your brain is well underway. I hope you realize by now that this is an adventure. You'll experience some starts and stops as you get underway, have some occasional layovers, yet always, your destination is a life of productivity, the life you've been yearning. Established habits of procrastination will take time to recede as you practice newer, better habits.

Keep me as a faithful friend, and return to the exercises you found helpful if you start to regress. As a fellow traveler, I have experienced the same frustrations you have, constantly putting things off and then suffering the consequences. That vicious cycle caused friction and kept me from reaching the goals I set for myself. I agonize and tried to change countless times, until I discovered these gems of wisdom and life hacks that changed my life. We suffered together, but now we are conquering together. Feel's pretty good, huh? Your challenge is to continue on that journey. Step by step, establish those new habits of productivity that will increase your self-esteem, decrease friction within your circle of influence, and maximize your earning potential.

Like you, I found change difficult but not impossible. The blueprint is yours and you are the master electrician. You and no one else gets to decide how your brain is wired. Remember to set goals to measure your progress, ensuring an ever increasing sense of self-esteem and a willingness to conquer procrastination for once and for all. I hope you're feeling empowered and ready to embrace this more productive lifestyle.

As you continue down this path, strengthening new resolves and abandoning destructive tendencies, you'll enjoy the many benefits in your relationships, in your career, and in your satisfaction with life. No more will conflict erupt when you put off taking out the trash as it overflows. No more will you put off sending out payments, incurring late fees. No more will you put off assignments with disastrous results. You'll see success in every avenue of your life.

Remember that procrastination is an addiction. Your addiction doesn't cost you money in purchasing items for substance abuse, but it costs you money in terms of productivity and achievement. Your addiction is destructive and you must summon up the will to overcome it. You may relapse at times and the tendency may ever lurk in the recesses of your mind. Give yourself grace. When you recognize a minor setback, forgive yourself. Dust yourself off and continue fixing you. Continue the process until your immediate response to any situation is the mindset, "I'll just do it. I'll do it now." You can achieve this. Your brain is yours. Wire it for top efficiency.